ENJOYING PROBLEMS

HOW LEADERS
GET TO THE NEXT LEVEL

DR. FRED RAY LYBRAND JR.

ENJOYING PROBLEMS

How Leaders Get to the Next Level

Copyright ©2024, Fred Ray Lybrand Jr. All rights reserved. No part of this book may be reproduced by any mechanical, photographic, or electronic process, or in the form of a phonographic recording; nor may it be stored in a retrieval system, transmitted, or otherwise be copied for public or private use—other than for "fair use" as brief quotations embodied in articles and reviews—without prior written permission of the publisher.

This publication is designed to provide accurate and authoritative information regarding the subject matter covered. It is sold with the understanding that the publisher is not engaged in rendering legal, accounting, or other professional services. If you require legal advice or other expert assistance, you should seek the services of a competent professional.

Design and cover art and formatting by RicaCabrex

Disclaimer: The author makes no guarantees of the results you'll achieve by reading this book. All business requires risk and hard work. The results and client case studies presented in this book represent results achieved working directly with the author. Your results may vary when undertaking any new business venture or marketing strategy

The best thing that can happen to a human being is to find a problem, to fall in love with that problem, and to live trying to solve that problem, unless another problem even more lovable appears. -Karl Popper

Contents

INTRODUCTION 1
Help Is Here. 3

PART I. 13

Chapter 1. The Power of Enjoying Problems 15

Chapter 2. Leaders as the Heroes of Problem-Solving . . 27

Chapter 3. The 7 Problems Successful Leaders Solve . . . 37

Chapter 4. The Secret Key to Mastering Your
Problems 45

PART II 59

Chapter 5. First Things First About Leadership
Anxiety 61

Chapter 6. The Lever: Erasing Leadership Anxiety 68

Chapter 7. The Simple6 Solution: The Only Moves
Needed to Solve Any Problem 75

Chapter 8. Solutions-Crafting with The Full Monty . . . 93

PART III 111

Chapter 9. Solutions-Crafting Step 1:
      Outthink Your Anxiety 113

Chapter 10. Solutions-Crafting Step 2:
      Discover Your Solution 127

Chapter 11. Solutions-Crafting Step 3:
      Design Your Plan 135

Chapter 12. Enjoying Problems as a Way of Life 145

CONCLUSION 155

What to Do Next 157
Appendix A: Fear as a Friend 161
Appendix B: Anxiety Outthinker Checklist 165
Appendix C: The Full Monty 167
Appendix D: Business Casual 171
About the Author 173
Bonuses To Enjoy 175
Additional Resources 177

INTRODUCTION

Help Is Here

May I share with you a secret to enjoying life even more, especially if you are a leader? One of my greatest sources of joy is helping you, as pioneers, remove your fear and solve your most pressing problems. Now, I have no idea what your most pressing problems are, but because you are human, I'm willing to make a bet. I bet they create the kind of stress and anxiety that stops you from seeing a solution or moving forward. I'm here to help you. Yes, you can remove your anxiety and solve your most pressing problems.

[As a means of reframing for those who respond well to a challenge, I am offering my opening words in each chapter in the style of a Mandalorian.]

> **Mandalorian**: *This is the way. Allow me to share with you a secret to relishing life to the fullest, especially if you are a leader. One of my most significant sources of contentment is aiding you, as pioneers, in vanquishing*

> *your fears and addressing your most pressing difficulties. While I may not be privy to the specifics of your most critical issues, as a fellow being, I'm willing to make a wager. I'm willing to bet that they create the kind of apprehension and unease that obstructs you from discovering a solution or progressing. Fear not, for I came to assist you. Yes, you have the power to overcome your anxiety and tackle your most pressing challenges. We will unleash it together. This is the way.*

Riddle me this...

What would it be like if you knew how to let the air out of your anxiety? What if you could happily get on to solving the problem in front of you without hesitation? What kind of team would you build if fear and anxiety didn't make decisions for you? What if they didn't even make recommendations? Probably like you, I'm an optimistic realist. I know that anxiety is everywhere because problems are everywhere. But what if you had a handle on anxiety and problem-solving such that your pressing problem was really nothing to fear? Applying the principles in this book, G.G. found a simple tweak which changed his worry and transformed his situation. He produced more profit in three months than he had in the previous year. C.J. accepted our help when he had one service truck. In four quick years he had five trucks and net profits beyond his dreams. L.S. embraced Step 9 of our process and created a way to redesign an international team. That team brought their company hundreds of millions in revenues. C.S. took our counsel and solved a key problem by dropping a category of customer. Yet, he still grew his profits to triple the year before. L.F. used our approach to completely end conflict between his teen sons. Once the solution was posted, there were no more conflicts while they lived at home. You'll learn about these as you continue reading. These individuals benefited from learning how to understand and solve their problems. They learned to craft better solutions. They found a better life by enjoying-and-ending problems forever.

Which brings us to the practical purpose of this book: To help you manage and remove your leadership fear and growing your confidence with better solutions. First, with a new state-of-mind skill, you will become free to solve your problems with an open, curious, and intelligent mind; unburdened by fear, worry, or concern. Next, when you solve your problem, any residual anxiety is gone for good. You can Enjoy Your Problems!

You may be wondering why we need another leadership book. More specifically, why am I writing this book? May I share with you how I got here? I've written nine books in my life, and with my diverse background, I still have the same basic reasons for writing every one of them. I studied communications and taught the same subject at the University of Alabama after graduation. I put some time in law school, but I wanted a career without having to have winners and losers. I moved on to get a degree in Bible/theology, and then pastored for 25 years. During that time, I started my coaching business so I could keep learning and understanding life outside of the church too. I focused on structural dynamics and systems thinking as it related to building businesses and healing relationships. During all that time I had to come to grips with my own struggles with anxiety. Every time someone wanted to talk to me, I kept wondering, "Have I done something wrong? Am I in trouble?" When you grow up in a house of alcoholics there's a good chance you'll have a few quirks in your personality. For the last decade I've worked with individuals, businesses, and organizations to help them get to the next level from wherever they were starting. **In every class, mediation, training, and problem-solving session, anxiety has always popped up as an undercurrent issue.** I bet it's there for you as well. Besides wanting to continue to learn, there are four basic reasons I've written this book:

- I want you to fulfill your purpose.
- I want to help you.
- I want us to change the world.
- I want to read this book myself.

Fulfilling your purpose is about faithfulness. Faithfulness is a loaded word with spiritual overtones, but I can't really hide that aspect of my life. I have a conviction that we are all here to play a role in this great act we call life. Our moment on stage is to be done well to honor the Great Director who set this all up. One way for our faithfulness to shine is to live with purpose and give according to our God-given talents. In fact, the original meaning of the word "talent" comes from a story in the Bible of three servants who were given large sums of money (talents) to care for while the owner was gone on business. When he got back, they were rewarded (or not) based on how well they multiplied the money. Your talents are not simply for your enjoyment, but they are for adding positively to this world on behalf of the One who gave them to you. You are a gift, and you are gifted. When you give from that place is where you find purpose. Your leadership role is a perfect opportunity for your talents and faithfulness to shine.

Next, I want to help you. Helping is a little nebulous, but it's nonetheless something that is hardwired into my soul. Now, I'll be blunt. My purpose here is to tell you the truth. When I do, you might think for a moment I'm not helping you at all! However, there's nothing quite so rewarding to me as seeing someone catch onto an idea, put it into action, and then see it change everything. My best guess from experience is that most people also have this theme in their soul, but they don't always find a good outlet for it. They help their friends, their family, their community, their school and so much more. I think that really is the idea, but occasionally we are allowed to see exactly how we can help on a larger scale. There's a famous movie from forever ago called Chariots of Fire. In the movie, the main character is supposed to go to the mission field, but he feels compelled to represent England in the Olympics because he was gifted to run fast. The famous line he utters is, "When I run, I feel His pleasure." In a similar way, I feel that "When I help, I feel His pleasure." Of course, I'm not trying to push anything religious on you here (or claim I'm an Olympian), but I think there is something about the human spirit that is beyond the mechanics of biology. Following your spirit is fundamentally spiritual, true? I don't meet leaders who don't want to help. So, equipping you to be anxiety-free and a wizard at solutions is a way to pass it on.

Third, I want us to change the world. I'm honestly not sure if I'm more interested in pain relief or promoting the ingenuity that makes our nation prosperous. In either event, the more individuals who know how to manage their anxiety and solve their most pressing problems, the more great leaders there will be. Moreover, these same individuals will experience more peace in their lives and more growth in their enterprises, departments, and businesses. How could it be any other way? You might be familiar with the story of the Fosbury flop, but maybe you're not. If you have ever watched the Olympics or a track-and-field competition, you'll notice that the high jump is approached by jumping with the backside over the bar. It wasn't always that way. In the old days competitors jumped facing forward. Dick Fosbury got injured because he couldn't jump well, and so he started pondering the mechanics of jumping to match the challenges he was facing. It also didn't hurt that he was a student of engineering. Once the flop was proved to be superior, the word spread, and today everyone uses the same technique. Imagine if we are onto something here about the connection between anxiety, problem solving, and getting to the next level as a leader. Word could spread and it could change everything! This could be your chance to be an early adopter, get ahead of the crowd, and be an example of transformation for generations ahead. By the way, don't you think Fosbury had to overcome some anxiety on the way to solving the high jump problem? You bet he did.

Finally, I want to read this book myself. Yeah, it's a little selfish. Years ago, I wrote a book on public communication that argued against extensive note taking and outline memorization. In my field of study, I could not find this book anywhere. So, after 10 years of research and reflection I went ahead and wrote it (search Amazon for Preaching on Your Feet)! In many ways this is the real reason to write any book; you just can't find it anywhere. I realize there's nothing new under the sun, but how it's said and what it emphasizes can be uniquely yours. I've never coached a leader or business leader who didn't struggle to some degree with anxiety and stress. I also know that they are all concerned about getting to the next level as they bump into the ceiling just above where they are. There are plenty of books out there on anxiety and there are even more books out there about scaling or business growth. I can't find a book that makes the real connection and explains that you must learn to master your anxiety so that you can then freely focus on your most pressing problem. This book is all about making that connection and helping leaders see the way out and up.

All of these reasons come to a simple focus; I want to help you achieve that dream that has gotten you into the thick of things. If you're like most leaders, the near experience is not one of taking a dive off the cliff. Instead, it's more like getting lost when you've gone on a glorious hike. You see where you're headed and you follow the trail, but then something happens. In a moment of disorientation or a fallen tree you step off the trail to solve the problem. But the problem leads to a new problem. You can't find the trail or your destination. It can feel like wandering, but with our bent to conquer, we press on. All the while your stress rises because the sun is beginning to set. You're not exactly worried about being a little lost, but a little lost can lead to walking off a cliff in the dark. Sure, you'd like to be back at the campsite, but mostly you just want to be back on the trail.

That's what I want to help you achieve, getting back on the trail. I can't imagine why you would have bought this book if you didn't feel the same way. Maybe you have cash flow problems or maybe you're so up to your rear end in alligators that you can't drain the swamp. Either way, the anxiety that comes with not exactly knowing the best next step is what interferes with finding the best next step. I want to help you achieve how to calm your anxiety so that you can think clearer. Once you can think clearly and add a few tools to your utility belt, you'll do what I like to call Outthink Your Problems. Of course, once you outthink your problems, then you can learn to enjoy them when they knock on your door.

There are only two satisfactory ways to deal with a problem:

1. You Can Solve It
2. You Can Quit Wanting What's Causing It

This book is about option one. Wants create problems, so this book will not help you if you just want to lie down and quit desiring successful outcomes (option 2). I've laid this book out in three simple moves:

- We'll understand how great problems are for our life and leadership, along with how they really work.
- We'll rethink anxiety and show you how to deflate it with your new understanding.
- We'll show you our revolutionary framework for tackling your problems as a leader and person.

My goal for you is to experience a dramatic drop in your anxiety before you finish reading this book. In addition, with being relaxed and focused, I also have the goal of you making great inroads in solving your most pressing problem.

After personally working with hundreds and hundreds of individuals over the years, I know that these goals are not too high for you, but rather belong to the common experience I have when helping people gain new insights and new skills.

There are three main points I want you to get from this book.

1. First, I want you to realize that anxiety can interfere with taking your best actions. Leadership anxiety is not unlike test anxiety, where you cannot remember the stuff you know. Leadership anxiety can keep you from solving the problems that are ready to be solved. Most of your anxiety is caused by misperceiving what's going on in reality. We'll fix that!
2. Second, I want you to understand the true nature of problems and how to define them accurately, so that they almost solve themselves.
3. Finally, I want you to understand how fixing your most pressing problem is the best way to end any anxiety. Most of the battle here is knowing how to approach a problem effectively. We'll fix that too!

Personally, besides the joy of helping others solve the pressing problems they have in life, I have experienced unusually better health for the past decade plus because of removing the bad kind of fears from my life. Stress really can be harmful, even deadly. My highest hope for you, the reader, is that you will complete this book and have a renewed confidence and passion for being the successful leader that you want to be. My hope is that you will learn to enjoy problems as you develop the skills you need, and then pass along your love for problems to others. As the wisdom I've collected in this book becomes clearer to you, you'll realize that what a book can do for you is powerful, but that applying these principles in person is 10X more powerful. I'll remind you again soon, but I'm a real person who works with real people to help solve their complex problems. If you'd like to experience the teamwork of outthinking a problem together, then just look at the additional resources at the end of this book. When you cure your anxiety and solve your problems, you can take your team to the next level and beyond. We're here to help you learn how to relax, focus, and happily overcome your next big problem. If you want to skip ahead, just drop us a note at support@enjoyingproblems.com

PART I

Chapter 1

The Power of Enjoying Problems

...when troubles of any kind come your way, consider it an opportunity for great joy. - James 1:2 (NLT)

I was lucky, but it wasn't luck.

It surely wasn't the first time I applied my 'enjoying problems' approach, but it probably was my greatest success. Over 40 years ago I met my wife Jody and asked her for a date. She turned me down because she was going out of town that weekend, so she said. I immediately asked her for a date the following weekend. She turned me down again saying she had to wash her hair or see a man about a dog or something. I hung up the phone and realized I had a problem. My problem was that I had a rule that I would not ask a girl out on a date more than three times. Suddenly I realized I only had one more shot. As I worked-the-problem, I came up with a solution that would guarantee she would either reject me or go on a date. My solution would be permanent and would leave no room for doubt. I went to the bookstore at the University of Alabama and purchased a calendar. It probably had puppies on the front or something like that. Next, I arranged to 'bump into her' on campus. I wasn't really stalking her; I just knew her pattern between the Tri-Delt house and the education building. "Hi Jody," I said. "Oh, hi Fred," she responded. "I bought you a gift." I handed her the calendar and she looked at me with that cute 'you're kind of weird' look I've seen throughout my life. I continued, "So, I've marked everything I'm doing for the next year in that calendar. If you would pick a date in the next year when I'm free, I'd like to take you out." Well, the rest is history. We've been married for over 40 years, have 5 grown kids, and 11 grandchildren (soon) under the age of 6 as of this writing. The solution appeared because of the way I framed the problem. I framed the problem because I knew what I wanted. All of that turned into a clear goal that gave rise to a clear plan…that worked! It doesn't exactly relate to leadership, but it does show the power of embracing problems and solving them. There are business-related stories of how I helped a cement company grow its net profits from about $250,000 to over $750,000 in one year. Another example involves how I played a solutions-catalyst role in getting a stuck pig unstuck under the North Sea (or some cold sea across the Pond), which resulted in an oil and gas company selling those assets for an undisclosed gazillion dollars. A pig is something used to scrape the inside of an oil pipeline to remove paraffin buildup to maintain flow. The stuck pig wasn't the actual problem, but once we figured out what they really wanted, the solution almost wrote itself. I didn't solve the problem, but our process helped the leader focus on a lasting solution. Kudos to the leader and kudos to the process.

Learning to enjoy problems will give you three specific benefits:

1. First, your anxiety will dramatically shrink away. Anxiety itself is a problem to embrace and solve. When it's out of the way, anything's possible.
2. Next, with a rock-solid approach, you can attack problems with confidence beyond your biggest dreams and toughest competitors.
3. Finally, your future will become more secure because your solutions work, and your problem-solving skills will keep you valued by those you can help.

A few days ago, I was talking to one of our clients about Thomas Edison and the mindset that he had in approaching each day. Instead of spending time on a variety of things like most of us do, Thomas Edison focused on the one problem he was working on that day. In large part, this is the reason he had 1093 patents including commercializing the lightbulb, the phonograph, the movie camera, and the distribution system for electricity. He thought something like, "The solution to a problem pre-exists and we will find it if we just keep working the problem." Perhaps even more importantly Edison knew what he wanted when he worked on a problem. He is famously quoted as saying he had not failed 10,000 times concerning the lightbulb, but rather that he knew 10,000 things that didn't work. Since I can't know what you are facing, I can't speak with authority. But I am confident that when you learn to clarify what you want, define the nature of the problem you face, and focus on finding the solution that is already in the wind, you won't need to try 10,000 things. In fact, you'll probably keep it under a dozen.

> **Mandalorian**: *This is the way. Remember, friend, problems are not adversaries to be feared. They are opportunities, gifts from the galaxy itself, which, when embraced, lead to growth and triumph. Embrace them, solve them, and your destiny as a leader shall know no bounds. This is the way. So, heed these words: trust in the process, for the solution exists, awaiting your unwavering dedication. Work the problem with unrelenting fervor, and you shall unveil the answer that shall set you free. This is honor, this is the essence of the way.*

One of the core strategies that we teach is the importance of seeking a permanent solution to any problem. Most of the time people stay in a cycle of experiencing pain, which drives them to take action, which lessens the pain, which lessens the action, which means the problem continues. Most problems are treated in such a way that they are like the baggage at Southwest Airlines; if you miss your bag the first time, it just keeps coming back around. In part this is caused by a poor definition of the problem, but more importantly it's the result of aiming too low.

In one of my past lives, almost 20 years ago, I took on the role of the pastor for a church which served around 1,500 people. When I showed up, we had two Sunday services and about 14 individuals in orange vests directing traffic between the services. The traffic was quite a mess and created all kinds of problems for us on Sunday mornings. One day I walked around the campus and thought about the problem. The temptation was to think about how to organize those directing traffic. In fact, I'm sure there are many things we could have done to improve the way traffic was directed. However, instead of trying to fix the traffic problem by improving our systems, I asked, "How can I completely remove the traffic problem forever?" My first solution was to build more parking spaces, which we did during multiple building projects. But, as I thought about it, I wanted the problem to go away right then. As I looked at the problem from this orientation, I expanded all the details I could look at and realized that the services were only 15 minutes apart. 15 minutes is not enough time to get your kids or to visit with friends or to get to your car. As a result, people were not leaving the church campus in time for newcomers to park for the second service. Even more important, I didn't want people rushing away from church. The obvious thing I finally noticed as I was thinking about a permanent solution is that the services simply didn't give enough time for the transition to occur. The moment we made the services 30 minutes apart is the moment that we needed zero individuals directing traffic. It's not that you can always find a permanent solution, but it does help shift your thinking in a profound way. Of course, you must learn to get over the fact that genuinely 'obvious' solutions will appear before you. You can think you are dumb not to see the obvious, but it's actually caused by using the wrong pair of glasses. Putting on the permanent-solution-x-ray goggles can open up a whole new world that will grow your enjoyment of problems. Also, when the solution is obvious, you really don't have to do much to sell it to others.

One startup company we helped had a problem in their programming department. This complex application that offers virtual physical therapy had been pieced together over the years by different contracted programming groups. Over the course of time, the basis of the application was what they called spaghetti code. Spaghetti code is a code that is a tangled mess that needs to be rewritten in a supported language so that everything works smoothly and is stable. When we came along, they mentioned that they had had it on their list as a project for some time, well over two years, in which they had not done one thing to fix the spaghetti code. They saw the problem as a project that they needed to get to someday. As we helped them work through our enjoy-your-problems framework, it became apparent that this was not something that needed a project orientation, but rather a constant improvement approach. We helped them design a simple process to have two programmers working at the same time on the same project but doing it one 'meatball' at a time. In other words, the lead programmer would figure out the next short-term thing to fix. Once it was fixed, they would come to agreement about the next meatball to fix. In this way they systematically built on each improvement. We also had them working at the same time, the same number of hours per week. These hours were sacred, but they weren't that many because of all the other bug fixes, etc., they were working on. In just a matter of months they began to see noticeable improvements in everything, including how quickly they could exterminate programming bugs. First, we aren't programming experts, so we weren't offering a ready-made template all programmers use. Their situation was unique to their goals and resources. Second, we didn't solve their problem. Instead, we played the role of a catalyst with our framework. You might say we drew the solution out of them, which is what you will experience with the process. You probably already have access to the answers

> **The solution I'm providing here is more than problem-solving, it's Solutions Wizardry.**

Learning how to enjoy problems and building the skills to solve them has changed my life in multiple ways. It's kind of like being a wizard who is focused on conjuring solutions for whatever comes his way. If the solution cures the problem, then the evil spell (the problem) is broken. Team members know I want problems, so we don't have awkward conversations where they're trying to keep problems from one another. Also, since personal problems, practical problems, relational problems, and leadership problems are just problems, our approach can be practiced all the time. Whether you are trying to track down problems or are just allowing them to show up (and they will), you are ready for action as you improve daily.

Here are 17 reasons to enjoy problems:

1. Problems lead to happiness.
2. Problems motivate us.
3. Problems make money.
4. Problems seek solutions.
5. Problems create jobs.
6. Problems give us purpose.
7. Problems create customers.
8. Problems grow skills.
9. Problems show us our strengths.
10. Problems reveal our weaknesses.
11. Problems create goals.
12. Problems show us what we want.
13. Problems create plans.
14. Problems inspire creativity.
15. Problems multiply learnings.
16. Problems unite people.
17. Problems exist anyway, why not enjoy them?

It may not be obvious why all these things are true, but we'll get to that so you can enjoy problems too. And, yes, they do lead to happiness. I guarantee it. I'm not the only one who's achieved these results. Here is another example from someone I've worked with:

The first time I became aware that having a strategic problem-solving framework can make all the difference occurred back in the day when there were one-minute photoshops. Before home printers and the Internet, there were expensive machines that could print quality photographs in an hour.

That was a bit of a big deal because usually you had to wait a week or more to get your photos printed. G.G. found me through a church, and we were just friends having coffee one day. He confided in me regarding his frustration with his employees not handling the expensive machines properly, not getting the quality they needed, and not getting photos printed in time. As I listened to him, I told him that I would define his problem in a very different way. I then told him the solution that made sense with my definition. I just shared with him how I would do things differently. Six months later at one of our coffee sessions he shared with me:

- I did what you said.
- I have amazing employees.
- I've netted over double the profits I had all of last year, in just six months this year.

G.G. began to change his relationship with his employees. He was more careful in hiring and had much higher expectations for himself as a leader and for his team members as technicians. Why? What did I tell him? I defined the problem as a hiring-quality problem, not a problem-employee problem. I just said that I would pay a lot more to his employees if they worked for me. He was paying them around minimum wage; probably because he just thought he needed warm bodies to work at the shop. I thought he needed quality individuals to run sophisticated machinery, and who would be motivated to stay with the job long-term (just training them took a while). On top of it all, it seemed to me that G.G. would be more particular in hiring and leading if he was paying more for their labor. Raising his pay scale alone began to transform everything for him. Of course, that was for his situation, but it holds up in principle for every situation. His life changed as a leader because he applied a solution to the real problem. You will see the same kind of transformation in your own success at a clearer definition of the problem you face. You'll learn how a better definition will give you a better solution in Chapter 8.

We'll look at this process in detail, but at the least you need to understand that your problem is solved by setting a goal that will solve it. Most of us have a default strategy of feeling pain and looking for relief. I call this 'problem-soothing' rather than problem-solving. It's like taking aspirin for leg cramps. It might ease the pain some, but it isn't really focused on a lasting solution for the real problem. Later on I'll show you exactly how to go from the pain and fear you are experiencing to a better definition, which means you'll discover a better solution.

I also used to problem-soothe in the old days. That meant I would experiment with a solution, find out it didn't really fix things, hear about another 'idea' and try it out. It was a constant cycle of try-fail-try-fail. No longer. Now I can frame the problem and solution effectively, so I pretty much know it's going to work. The only challenge I have now is making sure the implementation is good (for myself and my clients). No matter what they tell you, great execution on a bad idea will never produce a good result.

Instead of problem-soothing, I work on understanding my fear and my pain. If they point to an imaginary fear, I outthink it, so it goes away. If fear and pain point to a real problem, then I know exactly how to formulate a goal that can permanently (usually) solve the problem. Next, I form a solid plan and get to work. If you have the right approach and improve your skills, it'll be 'fun' to have problems cross your path. Yes, you'll learn to enjoy them in due time.

It all begins with a simple decision to stop avoiding problems and learning how to enjoy them. With a solid process that works, you'll grow to see how this gap in your skill set is the primary reason you aren't getting to the next level. It's not the competition, the customers, the marketing, the sales-pitch, or a crummy economy. In fact, it's nothing outside of you. It's you and the next-level skill you'll improve and enjoy every day for the rest of your life. Decide to be a master of solutions and you are on your way.

Let's see where you are right now. It's a simple No-Sometimes-Yes scale. Look at each of the statements and answer yes, no, or sometimes. Be honest.

1. I am restless and tend to fidget a lot when I am thinking about my team.
2. I am avoiding working on something important to the organization.
3. I keep thinking about something bad happening in the future.
4. I feel nervous most of the time.
5. I seek out distractions to give myself a break from thinking about my team.
6. I am more irritable than I'd like to be.
7. I have trouble relaxing.
8. I am not able to stop worrying about my team.

Chapter 1 Takeaways:
- Enjoy problems because of how great it feels to solve them!
- Enjoy problems for the 17 reasons we shared.
- Don't problem-soothe because of the pain, problem-solve because of the future.
- The better your skill, the more fun problem-solving will be.
- You need, but you don't yet have the skills needed to unleash them. We'll fix that too!

Chapter 2

Leaders as the Heroes of Problem-Solving

What led me to enjoy problem-solving, and why leaders? It was my natural inclination to solve problems, which has saved me again and again. And leaders are the right daring trailblazers to invite to join an adventure. Let me frame this in the style of a Mandalorian.

> **Mandalorian**: *This is the way: I have always been drawn to the art of problem-solving - a skill that has saved my skin more times than I can count. As for leaders, well, let's just say that their resilience and resourcefulness in the face of adversity have earned my respect. They are warriors of a different kind, fighting battles in the boardroom and on the front lines of commerce. But what is it that sets them apart from the rest? Join me on this quest, and together*

> we will unravel the secrets of problem-solving and leadership, forging a path to victory that is truly worthy of the Mandalorian name.

The purpose of this chapter is to help you determine if this book is for you. Frankly, I have a tough time imagining why someone wouldn't love to solve problems (if they really learned how to do it). Then again, I'm focused on leaders. These are the pioneers. By starting or growing a team, they take on the titanic challenge of changing their world. I enjoy problems. About one-half of all businesses fail in the first five years. So, I see a wonderful opportunity for creating solutions that matter. We can change the failure rate for most businesses. Your world can start out bad, but then turn to good. In fact, that's been the story of my life. Solving problems is the lifeblood of leadership. You embraced your role to solve a problem for a specific purpose. You hire people to solve problems for you, for the people you impact. A successful team solves problems for you. Your team gives you purpose and opportunity, as it provides for your family and your charities. Each part of the team impact overlaps with problems to solve in operations, marketing, finance, and new product development. If you get super-skilled at problem-solving, the future will be so bright that you gotta wear shades.

Problem-solving is the way leaders succeed.

I was born into a family with problems. OK, who isn't? But even to this day, extended family members don't like to think about what has happened in our families. I would never intentionally embarrass anyone, but it seems important to share a little of my story so you can understand why problem-solving is so personal to me. Is that OK?

I loved my mom and dad, grandparents, and aunts/uncles, etc. But many of them were alcoholics. They had more challenges than alcoholism, including secrets that probably deserved jail-time, medication, or a whole lot of private counseling. Nonetheless, I just want to mention the alcoholism. Some of the family courageously overcame the problem, but others did not. For at least part of their lives, though many died from it, mom and dad and grandmother and grandfather and grandfather all were challenged with drinking way beyond sanity, day-to-day, for years and years. Really, that's all you need to know. You are welcome to read books and pore-over checklists for adult children of alcoholics and codependency. I think I had them all! In other words, I was born, baptized, and bathed in problems. There was a lot of good around me, but since dad was also in the state legislature, my world had the priority of making things look good on the top while hiding the rotten underbelly.

I learned to enjoy problems. What else is a person to do? Externally I had to succeed (Eagle Scout, model citizen, successful student), but internally I lived with the morbid fear that everything would fall apart. I assumed I was in trouble in every situation and conversation, though I really was a fairly good kid. In college, things began to collapse with my own abuse of alcohol and relational dysfunction.

The good news is that I got better and was sent on a quest. In a way, I felt like the character in Monty Python's Holy Grail movie who condemns a witch for turning him into a newt. The crowd peered upon him as a whole man and he added, "I got better." That's it, I got better, and you can too!

Jean Le Rond d'Alembert was a French mathematician, philosopher, and physicist who was raised in a foster family and observed:

> *The difficulties you meet*
> *will resolve themselves as you advance.*
> *Proceed, and light will dawn, and shine with*
> *increasing clearness on your path.*

Maybe the hard way is a necessary ingredient, but I find this French dude's point to be my experience as well. In college, it became a spiritual awakening that led me to study theology, philosophy, counseling, and systems on the way into the light and on a clear path. My first career, as I've mentioned, was to shepherd people in the context of the church. For many years, my day-to-day work included three or more counseling sessions every day. In the course of time that led me to understanding family systems (Satir), which led me to organizational systems (Senge), which led me to structural dynamics (Fritz). In the due course of time, I learned to enjoy creativity and problem-solving, subjects people write about at length without giving us the real-world tools we need for leadership and life. Pretending children are great creators and problem-solvers is a grand faux pas in many popular books on the subject. What child creates a symphony or builds a successful international company?

They are curious, but without the guidance of wise adults, curiosity can kill them too.

Maybe your world was problem-free as a child, but is it now? How is your team, your relationships, your communication, and your leadership? If everything is clicking along like a well-oiled machine, then you won't really get much from this book. You'll just say, "I knew that...that's what I figured out...or, even...nah, that's way too simple." On the other hand, if you have come to realize that life is a journey of constantly overcoming problems, then welcome home. Is your problem limited resources? How about hiring good people? What about managing your time, especially overcoming procrastination? These kinds of real-world problems are common to us all, but they are not commonly solved. I believe the reason is that we are looking for solutions outside of our own skills and intuition to solve them. We keep looking for a book, a program, or a guru to hand us a paint-by-numbers solution. The weak link, however, is that your situation rarely matches the solutions they package. I'm open to being a guru, but I think I'm more in line with an old saying, "Christianity is one beggar telling another beggar where he found bread." This isn't a book about faith, but rather that I'm one problem-solving beggar who wants to share with you where he found bread. I'm not going to give you a fish, I'm going to show you how to build a fish factory.

Before I learned how to really enjoy-and-solve-problems in a permanent way, I commonly avoided them. There's another old saying, "You are enslaved by what you deny." Boy are those true words. **My greatest problem was to pretend the problem would go away if I ignored it.** I'm sure that works sometimes, but not normally. It's better to know about cancer early. It's better to realize where your bank account really is instead of hoping things are OK. Avoiding a tax problem only makes the tax problem grow. It's the same with debt, conflict, and addictions. As Barney Fife used to say, "Nip it. Nip it in the bud." My follow-up mistake after avoiding a problem was to just take some desperate action before thinking things through. Just after that, I'd make the third mistake of brainstorming ideas before I really understood the problem. In some ways, that was the most foolish thing I did. Randomized brainstorming feels good (hey, you have all these ideas!), but if they are not directed toward a solution to the problem at hand, they just become another bad idea. Imagine doctors brainstorming about a sick liver and deciding if they just remove it like a tumor everything will be fine. "Let's try that," they will say no more after the patient dies. **Coming up with lots of ideas and just doing something is probably the majority approach to problem-solving, and it almost always guarantees useless results.**

What was my life like before I started enjoying problems and using our problem-solving framework? The best I can say it involved a lot of experimentation and a lot of procrastination, so called. Just getting myself to focus daily was almost impossible. I had a problem I needed to solve with marketing and cashflow and just being productive. Nonetheless, I avoided working on things to my own harm. My debt grew to over $100,000 dollars (I have no debt now). When I did get around to working on a problem it usually helped. In fact, getting over problem-anxiety is more than half the battle. Then again, having a systematic way to understand and solve problems was where the magic happened. Of course, nothing is flawless in this world, but every day is a growing joy as I embrace my problems and conquer them systematically.

The turning point came when I discovered that a goal is just a solution to a problem. That might not sound like much, but most gurus on goal-setting and problem-solving set these things up as combatants. I often felt I needed better goals, but I was too busy solving problems. When I discovered how to fit both together the magic began. These were not enemies, in fact, they weren't even friends. They were the same hero that I had hallucinated were Dr. Jekyll and Mr. Hyde. There was no Dr. Jekyll, and the other guy came out of hiding! Solutions-Crafting is the super-power for a lifetime of success. If you grow that skill, what you want becomes possible, even likely. Of course, if you are crazy it won't help (just ask Dr. Jekyll).

Today, I'm debt free and more focused than ever. I enjoy rising early to get at the happiness brought about by working on the problems I've learned to enjoy and conquer. More to my own heart, my clients are an even bigger joy. I work as a solutions catalyst and help them solve their problems as they learn the skill themselves. Helping others is a deep value to me personally, and there is nothing quite like seeing lives transformed as problems end.

The biggest improvement I've seen in my own experience is that I don't look for the NEXT TRAIN. What I mean by this is that I'm no longer investing in one program after another looking for the Silver Bullet or the next station that has all the answers. Leaders don't follow fads, they follow principles. Everyone told me that if I just 'modeled' my life after them and followed their 'system' all would be well. What I discovered is that I'm not them. I'm not saying that I didn't learn a lot or gain a lot of value. What I am saying is that I couldn't remove myself and my situation from the process. Solving my problems with another person's solution never worked for me. I doubt it will ever work for you either. Even if you own a franchise, you'll have to solve problems unique to your shoppe, in your city, on your street. Frankly, there are four improvements I've seen since learning to enjoy my problems:

1. I quit chasing-and-hoping the next program would work.
2. I got focused.
3. I got productive.
4. I got even happier.

As William Blake wrote:

> *I must create my own system*
> *or be enslaved by another man's.*

What I'm really teaching you in these pages is how to overcome your anxiety and learn to enjoy problems, because you'll know how to strategically attack each one with confidence as you grow the most important skill for your life and success.

If you want to move your team forward, learn to enjoy your problems. Don't fret, worry, or delay. Your own anxiety is the first problem to solve, and I'll show you how to win over worry. Next, get ready to see problems in a whole new light.

Your problems are your way to success. They are not IN the way; they ARE the way.

My primary goal is for you to learn to dance with problems. Well, it's a way to picture it. Haven't you seen (or been) a young teen at a dance where you hang against the wall because you don't know how to dance? It's the same challenge with problem-solving, except you probably think you're pretty good at it, but still stay against the wall. Pause, be honest, and look at your results. If they are stellar, then you may not need what you are about to learn. If your results are lacking, here's your dance manual. If you get the idea and start practicing, you'll never be a wallflower again.

It is my hope that by teaching you how to outthink your anxiety and your problems you'll be able to quickly move to the next level. When you succeed it's hard for your team not to succeed as well.

Are you successful? I mean, if people looked at what you've accomplished would they say, "Yep, you've got a growing team. Way to go!" If they would, that's great, but you know more than they know. You know that you are stressed more often than you'd like. You know there are things to do, and they could mean a lot for your growth, but something is slowing you down. Do you feel like you are on the brink of something bigger, but it isn't quite happening? Well, you are exactly who I have in mind for this book. Would it help managers and leaders in larger businesses and organizations? Absolutely. Would it help startup leaders? Of course. However, the book is especially written for you if you are doing OK, but also want to get to the next level. It's also written for those who would like to experience a lot less stress on the way up. If that's you, keep reading. You can be a hero to your customers, your employees, and your family. Every problem you solve for them makes you the hero they hope for. Now, let's get specific.

Chapter 2 Takeaways

- Leaders are heroes.
- The way Leaders succeed is by solving problems.
- Your past gives you important lessons for your future.
- Hope and happiness are ahead for those who learn to master their problems.

Chapter 3

The 7 Problems Successful Leaders Solve

Let's talk about what you're facing. Frankly, it's going to be unique to your situation, just like the solutions you are going to invent.

> **Mandalorian:** *This is the way: The challenge you're up against is no easy feat, that much is clear. But fear not, for you are a warrior of your own destiny, and the solutions you seek lie within you. No two battles are alike, and neither are the solutions that arise from them. It is your unique perspective, your skills, your intuition, which will guide you to victory. So, let's get to work, let's forge a path forward, and let's discover the solutions that will pave the way to a brighter tomorrow. The way may be uncertain, but with the*

> *power of problem-solving at your side, you can face anything that comes your way.*

But, over the years of mentoring and coaching, there are some common themes. The first thing to notice is that you are not alone. You are not crazy. The same stuff is happening to almost everyone in your situation. The second thing to notice is that these problems are a defense against competition. When you get to a certain level you can see that it wasn't easy. You've already proved that you can endure and learn. Newcomers can't easily come in and sweep away your role and impact. In fact, most of them get swept out of your way early on (or they decide to learn from you). The challenge is for you to solve these problems shared by all leaders. If these problems remain, you'll stay where you are. In case none of these apply, don't miss the principle. **Your unsolved challenges are why you continue to stay where you are**. Also, it's an inside-out job. As I like to point out, it's hard to think crooked and walk straight. Your problems are real. But, your thinking and your skill-set are what's underneath them. In fact, you can accidentally keep your problems alive. Before we get to some answers, let's quickly acknowledge some common challenges leaders face.

1. **I'm Too Stressed and My Anxiety is Getting in the Way**

   This is where it all starts and ends. If you aren't anxious at all, then you are just a fool. Totally fearless people are stupid, and they do stupid things. That's not you. Anxiety is part of the path to wisdom, the path to knowing what to avoid as well as what to do. However, stress and anxiety can get the best of us. When you get anxious enough you can't think straight and you indulge in unhelpful 'relief' strategies (drinking too much, buying stuff you can't afford, going on trips you can't justify, and obsessing on sports, politics, or porn… just to name a few). If you are not there, then great. If you are there you need to wake up. These things can be poison to your spirit and your life.

Anxiety can lead to panic, and both lead to shutting down our prefrontal cortex. This part of our brain is where good thinking happens, especially something they call cognitive flexibility. When you can think clearly, you can come up with options and rate their probability of success. When you're too anxious you just get into the flight, fight, or freeze mode of operation. It makes sense. If you are strolling along in your neighborhood (assuming you live in the Central Indian Highlands) and a Bengal Tiger confronts you, the last thing you need to spend time doing is thinking through your options. Your brain is designed to save you, so it's going to compel you to take quick action. Unfortunately, this same effect can happen when we misperceive a drop in sales as a 600-pound killing machine. **When you learn how to calm your anxiety, you can think in profoundly more effective ways.** Most people don't really know how to handle their anxiety by outthinking their stress. Humming, breathing, and imagining your happy place can only give you a momentary break, if that. Once you think better about the cause of your anxiety everything changes.

2. I'm Just Too Busy

Busyness is the most common thing I work on with my clients. It's not only a complicated world with thousands of info-bits coming at us, but just the daily grind of making things work can suck the time and energy out of our souls. You probably started a business or moved up in leadership so you could be in control of your time, but your time is on you now. All day, into the night, and with the nagging responsibility behind your eyeballs, you keep thinking you'll take a break after you finish this next project. Face it, you gave yourself a new position and you can't easily ask yourself for time off. While this is best solved with systems and processes, it too is fundamentally a thinking problem. The way you understand and approach your team drives your decisions. **Problems are often soothed, but they are seldom solved.**

3. I Keep Working with the Team, But Not on It

Busyness leads to the neglect of your most important priority, working on the business. When I taught communications at the University of Alabama, I showed students how being involved in a team discussion works against team effectiveness. One of the simple tricks is to have one member sit in a corner and watch the meeting. A few years ago, an energy firm hired me to improve their meetings. We were able to take them from 1.5 hours per meeting to 45 minutes each. When you have up to twelve engineers + geologists + land people + environmental specialists meeting together several times a week, it can get rather costly. I simply observed and charted the interactions in the meetings. We came up with a simple design that got to the heart of accomplishing what they needed to accomplish. In other words, we worked on their meeting, not in it. All enterprises have the same problem. Basically, you need to realize that "It's hard to read the label from inside the bottle." Getting yourself free and focused on improving your effectiveness can be a dramatic step forward.

4. **I Can't Find a Good Path to Scale**

   Scaling up is the in thing these days, especially with entrepreneurial leaders. Scalability affects valuation, which affects selling the business someday. It's the same for team effectiveness. Scaling, however, can be a problem if you move too fast or make the structure top-heavy. Maybe this kind of lingo is new to you, but all we are talking about is how to get the thing to grow. It sounds easy. Entrepreneurs need to get more customers, cut costs, and add new products to sell to the old customers. Team leaders need to get the right people to do the right things, together. All that sounds fine, but the problems inherent in each of these can be insurmountable; especially if you aren't defining the problems correctly. Nonetheless, what could be more important than growth? Grow or die, right?

5. **I Can't Find Good People to Hire**

   Nothing is more common, or perhaps more important, than hiring and keeping good people. You hire problems when you hire the wrong people. It isn't easy, especially if you are in a competitive market where people are opting out of working or are climbing the tree of better pay. Even if you can find plenty of applicants, are they competent? If they are competent, do they have good character? Hiring an incompetent person who is 'good' can be as miserable as hiring a competent person who is bad. You hire people to solve problems, but if they cause more problems than they solve it's a bad move. Worse yet, your employees are the means to happy customers. If you don't hire good people, it can cost you far more than just their wages. Hiring can be a knotty problem, so problem-solving skills take the forefront on this issue. You can blame the culture (those millennials!), but you are better off blaming your solution that isn't working.

6. I Can Find Plenty of Ideas, But Not a Clear Direction

If you are creative, more power to you. But this isn't always the answer you want it to be. There are more articles, books, blogs, programs, and consultants than you can shake a stick at. Ideas abound, but which to use and where to go can be elusive. The first time I went to Six Flags (over Georgia) as a boy, we went into an ice-cream shop that had a couple of dozen flavors. This was way back when I had only known three: vanilla, chocolate, and strawberry. I was so overwhelmed with the options that I meekly said, "Vanilla please." Wow. Isn't that what can happen when you have idea after idea after idea? If that's not your challenge, then maybe it's trying out an idea that doesn't work before you see another idea to try. This endless cycle can be as exhausting as it is for a puppy chasing leaves in the backyard on a windy autumn day.

7. **I Have Plenty of Resources, But I'm Not Really Using Any of Them**

   Well While this is like the point above, it's the addiction of many serial leaders. There is a verse in the Bible that talks about "…always learning, but never coming to the knowledge of the truth." That's sort of the idea here. Programs are commonly built in a moment in time. They hit a niche or an approach and lay out the steps. If you follow them it might work, if you are quick enough. Yet, these things are often built on practices, not principles. Even in corporate America the notion of 'best practice' all-but-guarantees you'll be average. The innovators who succeed are creating the 'best practices' of the future, they aren't following them. You'll find as you improve your problem-solving skills, that a principle-based, innovative solution you invent is priceless. You probably don't follow someone else's plan because it either doesn't make sense or doesn't quite work in your world. Good for you to recognize that, but isn't it time for you to create your own program for your own team? Finding good mentors and coaches that can help you think precisely about your challenges can be worth their weight in gold. In some ways, having a mentor is like finding a good programmer rather than just a good program. There is a different level of accountability that comes along with insights, so a live resource can make all the difference in the world.

There you have it. The 7 big problems successful leaders solve. Here's a different way to emphasize the point. Imagine being a Team Lead or a business owner who:

- is not overly stressed or anxious.
- is not too busy but likes to work hard.
- works on the business, but not in it that much.
- has scaled his business well.
- finds and hires good people.
- has a clear direction.
- gets the right support for the right results.

How would things go if all this were true? You start with the Secret Key in the next chapter.

Chapter 3 Takeaways

- You're not alone.
- All leaders have similar challenges.
- Anxiety is an important first problem to conquer.
- Solving your problems comes easier as your skill improves.

Chapter 4

The Secret Key to Mastering Your Problems

The Secret Key to mastering your problems and growing your team begins with a decision. **Decide to quit solving problems and start creating solutions.**

> **Mandalorian**: *This is the way:* The secret key to mastering your problems and growing your team is not as elusive as some might believe. It all begins with a simple decision - a decision to leave the old ways behind and forge a new path forward. You must decide to quit solving problems and start creating solutions. For too long have you have been chained to the never-ending cycle of problem-solving, trapped in

a web of frustration and despair. But there is a better way, a path that leads to freedom and success. You must embrace the power of creativity, of innovation, of taking risks and making bold choices. So, make the decision today, abandon the flawed way of problem-solving and let the power of Solution-Crafting lead you to the success you so rightly deserve. This is the way.

Rethink your role and life. Replace problem-solving with solution-creation. This may sound like a contradiction, but it's the biggest reason leaders fail to solve their problems. You can add engineers, managers, and some football coaches to the list as well. When you focus on traditional problem-solving, you can easily fall into two of many traps:

1. Don't-Want Thinking Trap
2. Root Cause Analysis Trap

I don't know of two things that can better move you off course and fail faster. Like drinking saltwater, you think it is helping. You are busy and hopeful while 'quenching your thirst', but it comes around to bite you in the backside.

Don't-Want Thinking is all about looking at problems in terms of what you don't want. I don't want to run out of money. I don't want to lose a customer. I don't want my employees to be upset. It is incredibly difficult to organize your focus around something you don't want. The main reason is that there are so many ways you can see that happen. As a result, you'll tend to bounce around with different short-term efforts. What you want is solutions focused, which we'll get to shortly. Just know that every time you express what you want as a 'don't want', you are muddling your thinking and your communication. It's one of the most pernicious tricks we play on ourselves to stay addicted to trying to solve problems the wrong way. When you shift to Do-Want Thinking you'll see a shift from just trying to solve a problem to new focus on creating a solution. The Secret Key is all about learning how to think better (way better) about your problems and follow a process that works. There's no more random luck required or hiring a specialist for the one thing you need.

We start with a fresh thought: Quit Problem-Solving. At first glance you may miss how this key is different. If you are an entrepreneur, you don't want to lose money, you can do that by spending less (but normally you can only cut about 10% anyway), or begging customers to renew, or shutting down the business altogether. If you don't want to lose a customer you can also beg, create a totally different time-consuming offer for them, or just keep apologizing for everything. If you are a team leader, you don't want your reports to be upset. You can expect less, not hold them accountable, and give them more time off to make them 'happy'. Do you see where this is going? You are problem-focused, and your process will never get you where you want to go.

Imagine being Solutions-Focused, that is thinking about what you do want. In that case you'd be asking questions like:

1. How do you increase revenues?
2. How do I gain more happy customers?
3. How do I build a happy and focused team?

Focusing on solutions transforms everything. I'm with Uri Levine (WAZE) that we shouldn't fall in love with our 'solution'. However, we do want to fall in love with the problem solved. Even in the day-to-day world of parenting you can see this power. Imagine your children are always fighting. If you want them to stop fighting (Don't-Want Thinking), you can send them to their rooms, a neighbor's house, or a military institute. But if you are thinking about a real solution you want, you'll ask, "How can we help you both cooperate and support each other?" I had this with two late-teenage sons who fought all the time. When I came to my senses and thought about Do-Want instead of Don't-Want, I came up with a plan. For the remaining year-and-a-half that they still lived together at home, they never had another fight. If you are interested in our approach to parenting and education, you can check out our stuff at https://independenthomeschool.com

Now, what about the **Root Cause Analysis Trap?** On the surface it seems to make a lot of sense. Hey, figure out the root cause of the problem and fix it. What could be simpler? The common notion of a root cause is that it is the fundamental cause when something happens. It's the thing to fix. No problem, right?

Well, the first problem is that there is no such thing as a root cause. In fact, for eons logicians have warned us about the *Root Cause Fallacy*. There really are no single-cause events of any kind (unless God alone created the universe). Even in manufacturing where there are steps in the process, declaring the root cause can still take the team away from real improvements. *The Root Cause Fallacy* is also akin to another fallacy called Hasty Generalizations. This fallacy is basically a rushed conclusion based on insufficient data. If you want to go full nerd, there is also the fallacy of the single cause, also known as complex cause, causal oversimplification, causal reductionism, and reduction fallacy. It's all basically the same. Proponents of Root Cause Analysis seem to think making causes plural changes the game, but it doesn't. Getting several 'root causes' is the same problem, exactly. Technically, there are no root causes; there is the cause itself, which is a dynamic of the elements involved. Looking for a root cause or causes is a path to misdiagnosis. So, when you misdiagnose the cause, you will misdiagnose the remedy. Here's an example. What is the cause of rain? Think about it. Is it water? Well, you can have 100% water in the air, but only see fog. Is it heat? No, there are deserts. Is it cold? No, there are cold deserts called tundra. Causality is systemic, which means that a number of things come together to 'cause' something to happen. Root Cause Analysis can lead to shallow thinking and shallow solutions. The process of discovering the root causes of problems in order to identify appropriate solutions just means you'll lock into a single idea that often has little to do with what you want. If the root cause of a lack of money is spending, then the solution is to cut costs and become miserly. If the root cause of lack of money is not enough advertising, the solution will be to advertise (often into oblivion). The success of your efforts will have multiple elements, not a root cause. It will turn out to be the same with organizational problems. They aren't about a root cause, but fundamentally about what you really want as a leader.

The second reason that Root Cause Analysis is so dangerous is that it is given to group dynamics and group think. One person can lead the group to conclude that 'one thing' is the root cause. In studies on this problem, it is commonly discovered that if the individuals are left to themselves apart from the group, a large variety of 'root causes' are offered. Deciding on the root cause can come from politics and persuasion, rather than the data and thought. Of course, whatever root cause is settled upon dictates the solution, so creativity is out the window. In the same way, if you make a hasty conclusion about what the problem is, you'll be off on a path away from the answer you seek. In group settings, root cause thinking is often a mechanism for blaming something so as to avoid responsibility. Yes, there are some contexts where root cause thinking makes sense, usually around a process. Factories have processes that make products. A piece of the process can break down, and so it is labelled the root cause. A cake can be ruined by using spoiled eggs, which could also be called a root cause. We encourage people to get away from this kind of thinking for the mere fact that you can miss something. If you use both spoiled eggs and spoiled milk, but decide it's just the eggs; well, you're off to the races (but you won't win).

Let's look at how the Secret Key got discovered and will help you thrive as a leader.

A prudent question is one-half of wisdom. – Francis Bacon

The most important question I've ever asked is "Why?" Well, I did ask Jody to marry me, so there's that. But "Why?" can take you to new vistas to see new lands. Yes, I was one of those, "Why is the sky blue?" kind of kids. As I aged, my 'why' questions moved to 'how' to make things happen, specifically asking, "Why does it work this way?" Why do mom and dad fight? Why is it snowing at my house and not at my grandparents? Why doesn't my fiction-writing professor like my poems? All of these led me to a second awesome question, "How?" How do you persuade others? How do you get an A in this class? How can I get Jody to say 'yes' to a date? You get the idea.

"Why is this a problem and how does it work?" I kept using that question and usually answered it like most people do on social media; with the first thing that popped into my head as obvious. Why do my political opponents think the way they do? They're stupid, that's all. Well, if you can think at all you know that the 'problem' is a little more complicated than that!

In the course of time, I realized that a more compelling question needed to be asked about problem-solving, "Why don't we focus on the solution we want?" It occurred to me that if I focused on what I wanted, and made it happen, then the problem would go away by default.

Years ago, I had a small backyard and Miss Scarlett, a large Doberman Pinscher. There was a wooden fence and a small concrete path next to it. The pain point was that my big dog would smell the outside world through a small knothole in the fence and her body would step out into the grass. Soon I had a bald spot of dirt where she was stomping. The problem was caused by my desire for grass. The driver was her nose, but I couldn't cut it off. I wanted her not to wear out the grass, so

I thought about putting up stakes and mesh to keep her off the grass. As I sat there and thought about it, while in a long-term mentoring program about structural dynamics (more about that later), I clarified what I wanted. I wanted her to be able to smell the outside world and I wanted the grass to grow. Obviously, if that hole was in a different place with no grass, the problem would be solved! I got a hammer and moved two fence slats so as to place the hole in front of our cast iron chiminea. Within a day Miss Scarlett was sniffing next to the chiminea and the grass was back in a week. Yes, it's a dinky example, but that's the domain of power. When you simplify things and can apply them anywhere, you are on a path of success. I enjoy problems and I want you to enjoy them too.

At this point you might be asking a few questions about why you should quit solving problems and start creating solutions. Let's see if we can outthink them.

1. **How is this different from regular problem-solving?**

   The most common way people solve problems is to react to the symptoms or the pain-points the problem is causing. This is a reactive strategy and almost always avoids a lasting solution. We come by this honestly. It starts out when we are babies. We have a problem, then we cry. Fortunately, most of us have parents and caretakers who look at the crying as a symptom. They then work to figure out if it's a wet diaper, a hungry stomach, or an earache, etc. But, what if like some dysfunctional parents, you think the crying is the problem itself? In that case, they will isolate the child or even put duct tape over its mouth. Cruel and criminal, but it comes from being a reactive problem-solver. Frankly, it could be that you are just putting duct tape on your own problem and putting it in a back room out of earshot. That's a common way regular problem-solving 'works'.

2. **Isn't creating solutions the same thing as solving problems?**

One of my mentors, Robert Fritz, makes a helpful observation when explaining the difference between creating and problem-solving. Creating is about bringing something into being. There is no chair, you build a chair, and now there is a chair. That's creating. Problems are more about something to remove. There is a fallen tree across the road, you remove the tree, and now there is no problem. It's overly simple, but it does get at the point. When you begin to understand that you can create something that solves a problem as a byproduct, then you are stepping up to a new level. In our example, if you wanted to guarantee a road never has fallen trees on it, you could build it on a bridgework so that it is above the tree line. Expense and reasons aside, focusing on creating a road on a bridge over the forest is bringing something into being that didn't exist before. By default, fallen trees are not a problem. Frankly, if you'd like to see this solution applied, drive over the third longest bridge in America, the Atchafalaya Basin Bridge in Louisiana (I-20). Your problems are bound to be a little easier and a little cheaper, but the idea is the same. **Creating something that solves your problem is** a different game than just trying to get something out of the way.

3. **I still want the problem to go away because I don't want it.**

    When we talk about problems in a day-to-day manner, we certainly say, "I don't want _____." However, we are looking at how to make the problem go away. It really isn't helpful to build 'don't want' strategies and goals because it isn't focused on a thing (it's focused on the absence of a thing). 'I don't want to be single' is less helpful than 'I want to be married'. Focusing on getting married leads to many effective ideas and actions. Not wanting to be single leaves it in the vague world of wishing. Not wanting to be broke is different than wanting to be wealthy. In leadership, wanting a great team helps far more than not wanting a bad team. Of course, you still don't want a bad team, but the focus for action is profoundly more effective when creating a solution to focus on building a great team.

4. **Are leadership problems really that different?**

    Aren't we all facing the same basic things? There is no doubt at the highest level of patterns we all face the same problems as leaders. We need R&D, marketing, and effective operations. Yet, since our businesses and situations are different, applying a generic solution really won't work unless it is solving for the same business and circumstances. In farming, this is why the soil gets tested. If you need nitrogen and add it to the soil and the crop is abundant, then great. If you assume the next time you need nitrogen when you really need iron, you will neglect the iron and poison the field with too much nitrogen. Principles are helpful, but we aren't all facing the exact same things. What works for me might not work for you, so it's best to be smart and outthink your unique problems by creating a targeted solution for your specific situation.

5. **I already think I know how to solve problems, it's just that some of my problems are impossible to fix.**

If you have a problem that is truly impossible to fix, then you don't have a problem. We'll look at this later, but realize that some things are just the reality you face. Problems, by their nature, can be solved. Realities, by their nature, just are. Reality is what you work with to solve the problems you can solve. This is what's behind the Serenity Prayer:

> **God, grant us the serenity**
> **to accept the things we cannot change,**
> **the courage to change the things we can,**
> **and the wisdom to know the difference.**

6. **Thinking about problems seems to be negative thinking, which is just the opposite of the positive thinking we leaders need.**

Problem-solvers are optimists because they believe that the problem can be solved. Optimism is great, but optimism that denies the facts in play is just another form of stupidity. Pessimism is also bad when one is hopelessly inactive. When Tom Brady faced the full length of the football field with less than two minutes remaining in order to win, he was the ultimate optimist and leader. That's the spirit of leadership. We learn to enjoy our problems like Tom Brady enjoyed the two-minute drill. It calls for our best!

7. **I have no problems in my situation that money can't solve.**

Money does solve problems. Then again, if you had enough money, you probably wouldn't be connected to a business. Money is the output of a business, it's not the solution to a problem. When you reinvest money to grow the business, it is still for the outcome of more money. Education is a good counterexample. It's ubiquitous that huge sums of money have been thrown at all kinds of educational problems, but the better facilities and programs often don't turn out better educated students. Money must be properly directed, so there's a problem to solve as well. If it's true that all you need is money, then that's the problem to solve, pointing to the solution to create. A solution-focused approach to problem-solving is catching traction in many areas of business and government, especially among those who treat solution-creation as a process to learn. One of the most dramatic impacts has been in the counseling arena. Most of psychology has abandoned Freud (except his thoughts on defense mechanisms) because of the dismal results and flawed explanations of mental and emotional problems. The old days of counseling just involved endless conversations about why the past has warped the client. Often, they turned in to brainstorming sessions about how to cope with any new 'insights' about the past. Fortunately, approaches like Brief Therapy began to look at counseling with a short-term, solutions approach. Instead of focusing on 'not getting a divorce' (a 'Don't Goal'), they began to aim the client at 'building' a better marriage. In time, some of the originators refined it to be named Solution Focused Brief Therapy. That sort of says it all, true? It's a movement away from problem-soothing to solution-creating.

Another major area where this approach has caught on is in computing. First, there was the growth of the user-friendly orientation. Programming shifted to have a solution for the end-user in view. Before that, programming was given over to the specialty-nerds who loved to get inside and rewrite the computer code. Agile came along next and approached programming from a let's-get-better-and-better method, but with the customer in mind. Creating for the customer has proved itself to far outweigh just solving problems in the code.

Chapter 4 Takeaways

- Quit solving problems and start creating solutions.
- Avoid the "Don't Want" Trap and the Root Cause Trap.
- A prudent question is one-half of wisdom.
- You can outthink your toughest problems.
- If reaching a goal will solve your problem, then do that instead.

PART II

Chapter 5

First Things First About Leadership Anxiety

The modern mental illness is anxiety. -Naval

Now you have a good idea of the power of solution-creating over problem-solving. You are catching on to how your instincts can sometimes lead you astray. And, you haven't yet learned our powerful approach for growing the skill of the century, Solutions-Crafting.

> **Mandalorian**: *This is the way: You have taken the first step, and that is to understand the power of solution-creating over problem-solving. You are beginning to see how your instincts can lead you astray, how the endless cycle of problem-solving can keep you trapped in a cycle of despair. But there is a better way, a way that leads to true mastery, a way that empowers*

> *you to craft solutions that truly make a difference. You have not yet learned our powerful approach for growing the skill of the century, Solutions-Crafting. It is a method that taps into your inner creativity, guides your intuition, your unique perspective, and channels it into solutions that are truly game-changing. So, heed my words, embrace the power of Solutions-Crafting, and let it guide you to the success that awaits. This is the way.*

Soon you will feel a new hope about old problems. But slow down. There is a challenge you must face down before you get into mastering your problems. If you miss this step, your odds of succeeding drop dramatically. It's not your fault that you can miss this step in the process. In fact, it is the driver behind the wheel of your efforts to solve your problems. We mentioned it before, but now it's time for a little more detail.

The first thing you must overcome before solving your pressing problem is any crippling anxiety. One of my mentors taught me something important about stress. He said that when stress hits the system, our pathology overrides our philosophy. What does that mean? It means that when you were growing up you experienced all kinds of events. Then you interpreted them in a certain way, sometimes a dangerous way. We can see this happen in certain situations, especially when we are around family members. Have you ever noticed how they can 'push your buttons'? They make you behave in ways that just aren't really you. The family can push these buttons for the simple reason that they installed them! These things that are programmed into our being are what we mean by our pathology. Here it's a compulsive 'path' we follow in times of threat or danger. As we mature and develop, we can conquer these tendencies. We can realize they may have served us well as kids, but they don't any longer.

When you are stressed and anxious about a problem you are facing, your brain will shut down your creativity and objectivity to solve your problem. Frankly, it doesn't have to be stress about the problem you are focused upon. It could be that you are stressed about your home life, but it keeps you from the clear thinking needed at work. Of course, it can go the other way as well. You can be anxious about something at work, and it won't allow you to solve problems at home.

It's easy to think that solving the problem will decrease your stress (and so it will), but you can easily miss the bigger picture of what your anxiety is doing to hinder your life. In a way, it's like the oxygen masks on Southwest Airlines. They are careful to explain that in the event of an emergency we are to put the mask on ourselves first, before attending to any children traveling with us. Why? It's kind of obvious because of the necessity of the sequence. If you are conscious, you can help your child. If you are unconscious, you can't help your child. It's the same with solving problems. If your anxiety isn't solved, your problem-solving won't be successful. I can't emphasize this enough. You simply must learn to be a chillaxed leader. It's essential to learning to enjoy problems.

Most programs out there do not make this intimate connection between anxiety and problem-solving. Some of them emphasize dealing with anxiety as an overall issue, but that could be applied to anyone (if their program even works). Others are trying to sell you their solution to your specific business problem or problems. Frankly, I think they are getting it all wrong. Conquering anxiety is intimately connected to inventing solutions unique to your situation, and both must be addressed. Really, we are talking about you developing the skill you need to assist you throughout your life. They are all about 'done FOR you', where I'm all about 'done IN you'. Of course, you will hire solutions and team members, but you must learn to calm your anxiety while being skilled at creating great solutions. Welcome home!

The biggest challenge you'll face in learning to create solutions, rather than focusing on solving problems, is believing it works. You see, mastering problems by creating solutions is counterintuitive. It seems obvious that you need to get rid of something rather than create something else that solves the problem. In a way, it's like learning to fly a plane by instruments. Pilots who crash when they are disoriented by something like a fog bank keep trusting how things 'feel' to them, rather than believing what the instruments are telling them. How can focusing on a goal instead of the problem really solve things? Well, when you outthink your problems, you can see the whole picture. But when you focus on immediate relief you can't see the forest for the pine-needles. Counterintuitive basically means counter-obvious.

Years ago, my oldest son, who happens to have mild cerebral palsy, got separated from his swimming partner at the beach. Suddenly he was in over his head and the rip currents were trying to take him from Gulf Shores to Cuba. We had just arrived at the beach. I was still dressed when Tripp's sister, Laura, hollered that he was in trouble. I gave my wallet and keys to my wife and started to strip down, all the while signaling for Tripp to swim to his left (with the current, not against it). I never got in the water. Shortly he was safely on shore. In these currents it feels like you are being swept out to sea, so your instinct is to swim against the current, which just exhausts you into drowning. I knew these currents from a lifetime at the beach, that they are still making their way to shore. Counterintuitively, I had Tripp swim with the current and all was well. As a leader, it feels obvious to do something to relieve the pain and anxiety in the moment. The counter-obvious answer is to create a special kind of solution that will solve the problem forever. You must learn to think this way, that's the challenge. We solve this problem by helping you build experiences that get it into your bones to live a life of solution creation by being wise and counter-intuitive.

The nagging problem with using the Secret Key of quitting traditional problem-solving is the leadership bent to constantly try new things. Most leaders get into a role because they love the excitement of the challenge. Unfortunately, this tempts us to keep trying different things until something works. While that isn't all bad, the problem is that we don't give a solution enough runway to take off. That's the danger with trying to relieve your pain by doing something short-term. Again, it's like drinking salt water. We solve this by getting you to focus on a goal that will solve the problem. If you are looking at a goal, then you know that you don't stop until you reach it. The goal-solution itself solves the problem, so you don't get distracted by asking if 'it's working or not'. Yes, it's simple, but it is an entirely new way to think and act. It also will change your life for the better once you quit merely trying to solve problems in your old instinctive way. Additionally, the reason this kind of solution-focus also works is because limits yield focus. When you have multiple options and multiplying ideas, there are just simply too many options. When I was growing up, we only had three channels on TV, and we milked them for all they were worth. Today, 'nothing' is on TV/Cable/Netflix/Etc. because there are simply too many options. There isn't a way to focus because there isn't a single choice (at least binge watching helps a little). When you dump all the options and put your efforts on the solution that will end the problem, you have a limit, and so you also have focus.

Finally, you must add one thing to make this Secret Key work for you. You must quit looking at the problem and set your face squarely at the solution you have ahead of you. In the climactic scene from the Lord of the Rings Trilogy, Frodo is barely hanging on to a ledge with lava bubbling below. Samwise pleads with him to reach up and grab his hand. Frodo could think about the problem of slipping off the ledge or he could think about reaching up for Sam's hand. Focusing on the ledge and the lava would have been a focus on the problem. Setting himself to reach up to a helpful hand was a focus on the solution he needed. Yeah, they made it! You are going to make it work for you too when you give up on the sporadic 'try anything' approach that sinks most leaders into the flame of failure. Learning to forge ahead to a solution that you have invented yourself will make you the hero you are meant to be.

Chapter 5 Takeaways

- If your anxiety isn't solved, your problem-solving won't be successful.
- The biggest challenge you'll face in learning to create solutions rather than focusing on solving problems is believing it works.
- The nagging problem with using the Secret Key of quitting traditional problem-solving is the leadership bent to constantly try new things.
- If you want to focus, quit looking at the problem and look at the solution, once you find it.

Chapter 6

The Lever: Erasing Leadership Anxiety

There is an essential in outthinking your problems and crafting solutions. You might think of it as a lever involving your mind and anxiety.

> **Mandalorian**: *This is the way. In order to outthink your problems and craft solutions, there is an essential tool that you must possess. Think of it as a lever, a simple yet powerful device that can move mountains. This lever is none other than your mind. Your mind is the most powerful tool at your disposal, capable of shaping your reality and conquering any challenge that comes your way. But like any tool, it must be wielded with care and precision. You must learn to use your mind to its fullest potential, to tap into your inner creativity, your better intuition, and your*

> *unique perspective, and channel them into solutions that are truly transformative. However, if your mind is filled with anxiety, it will cause you to hesitate, and it can lead you astray. So, remember this: the lever of your mind overcoming anxiety is the key to unlocking the power of Solutions-Crafting, and the path to true mastery. This is the way.*

Sometimes it's more like Dr. Frankenstein's lever: A switch that sets in motion shooting electricity through the monster's body to bring it to life. Maybe your team needs a jolt for monster results? Personally, I think it's more like Archimedes' point:

> **Give me a lever long enough, and a place to stand, and I will move the entire earth.**

Getting your anxiety to calm down opens the door to creative thought. It's important to understand this concept, so endure a minute or two of nerd-speak. A lever is about leverage, which is basically a mechanical advantage. Practically, it's about a small effort to produce a big result. Everything you do or experience has leverage in play. All the pieces are not equally influential. Ten good reviews of your enterprise can be erased by one bad one. Bad reviews have leverage. The influence of a bad review can do far more harm than a good review can do good. A sharp axe can cut a tree faster than a dull one. So, sharpening the axe is leverage. Pareto discovered the 80/20 Rule, which realizes 80% of sales come from 20% of customers. Also, 20% of customers produce 80% of the problems. Two team members influence a team of ten more than the remaining eight. Leverage means everything isn't equal in its influence, but it doesn't mean the others aren't important. When you see the principle, you can look for the leverage.

In solving your problems by creating solutions, anxiety is the essential leverage-point in the process. **Ending Anxiety is the Lever.** If you calm your anxiety, you will increase your ability to solve your problems. That's leverage. Just like a bad online review, having anxiety can stymie your success in crafting a solution. Even if you have an OK process, you'll never use it effectively if you are anxious and over-stressed. Of course, some anxiety is good, but that's not what we are talking about. Anxiety for the leader is fear gone wild. When fear goes wild it shuts down our ability to think and act wisely. If this isn't you, then skip ahead. But, before you skip ahead, why not take a quick inventory of your feelings about your challenge, especially your hopes and dreams. I have a good friend who built a great energy business with a few of his friends. One time he told me that starting a business was great once you got over being bothered about throwing up in the shower every morning! That is anxiety. Finding oil & gas is high stakes and you can go under easily. That was his point. Having a problem go away definitely can reduce your anxiety (more about that later), but **anxiety needs to go away before you start working the problem**. Like test anxiety, you can flunk even if you know your stuff.

I call the lever here the Anxiety Outthinker. There are a variety of techniques, but it all comes down to one thing: outthinking your anxiety. Anxiety can be specific, but it's really the overall tendency we have to worry about everything, to see things threatening us everywhere. Maybe you don't resonate with global anxiety in your life, but if you aren't given to a fair measure of stress, you probably aren't pursuing much success. Of course, if you know how to outthink your anxiety, then that's a different game altogether.

Here's how it works. When you are upset there is a basic cause. You are upset because you are thinking upsetting thoughts. That is what is really going on. It's simple, but it's not simplistic. It's not about deep issues between your Id, Ego, and inner child. It's also not a root cause. But it is where the leverage lies. **You can erase your anxiety by outthinking the thoughts that are haunting you.** It might be more accurate to say that you scribble over your upsetting thoughts, but either way your emotions won't read them as anxiety-worthy.

It's not what is happening that stresses us, it's how we think about it. Rain is a good example. Imagine it raining just as you are crawling into bed on Sunday night after a good weekend. How do you feel about the rain? It's probably soothing as you drift off to sleep. Imagine a farmer who is a few weeks from total crop failure because of a long drought. If it starts to rain, he will probably dance in the front yard! But imagine a young bride who is having an outdoor wedding. If a deluge starts the moment she is walking down the aisle, she'll probably be pretty upset. **How we interpret what's happening is the foundation, the lever, which allows us to outthink anxiety any time, any place.**

Anxiety is a reaction to how badly we imagine the future being. Depression, in contrast, is how we negatively imagine the past. When you imagine something happening in the future that you don't want, all you can do is be anxious. If you aren't anxious about something bad happening that you don't want, then you are crazy. What if we could erase your prophecy about the unwanted future? Wouldn't your anxiety dissolve? I assure you that is exactly what would happen, and I'm going to show you how to do it. In a nutshell,

1. You want to imagine two additional alternative futures that are possible.
2. Next, stand them alongside the future event you fear.
3. When you realize all three futures are possible, then your anxiety must collapse. It must collapse, because you can no longer be sure about the one bad future you've imagined.

If you aren't sure the future will be bad, you can't worry about it in the moment. I'll soon walk you through the process in detail.

We are not talking about hypnosis, psychology, or NLP. We are talking about learning how to direct your thinking, how to outthink your anxiety. Nonetheless, a skilled individual can help you learn to run your brain 10X faster, but it isn't counseling, it's coaching. If you want to learn more about our in-depth training, then start by getting the free resources offered at the end of the book. I know at this point I've shared a lot of information about problem-solving and erasing your anxiety. It's easy to think you can't grasp all of this, but fortunately it's written down. You can absolutely learn what you need here because you can review it all you want. More to the point, you really want to embrace a truth that will turn you into a persistent learner:

> **Everything is hard before it's easy,**
> **but it's easy once you know how.**

Don't give up, and don't slow down. We are about to get to the especially practical part of the book. I assure you, however, that understanding the insights above is vital. Up to this point you have been learning 'why' we take the approach we take. If I had started with 'how' to do it, you'd be asking, "Why?" But, since I began with 'why', you are wondering, "How?" That's exactly where we are headed.

Chances are you've tried a few things before reading this book. In fact, you've probably had training on creativity or problem-solving somewhere else. I'm sure that's true; me too! It is rare for the programs I've studied to give me the complete solutions I needed. The reason is simple; they were too vague or too specific. In that middle range is a way to learn that is principle-based. Principle-based means the approach can be applied to a multitude of situations. When you found this book, you found a principle-focused solution. I'm not sharing a list of cliches for you to mimic, nor am I giving you a perfect step-by-step that can only be used at work. I'm sharing a thinking process with an action sequence that can turn you into your own problems mastery specialist. Keep reading and you'll see why I can make such a claim. Face it,

> **If you knew how to solve your problem,**
> **you probably would have already.**

You are at a fork in the road. As Yogi Berra liked to say, "When you come to a fork in the road, take it!"

Chapter 6 Takeaways

- Getting your anxiety to calm down is the key that opens the door to creative thought.
- You are upset because you are thinking upsetting thoughts.
- Anxiety is a reaction to how badly you imagine the future being.
- Depression is a reaction to how you negatively imagine the past.
- How you interpret what's happening is the lever that allows you to outthink anxiety any time, any place.
- If you aren't sure the future will be bad, you can't worry about it right now.

Chapter 7

The Simple6 Solution: The Only Moves Needed to Solve Any Problem

Let's look at the Solutions-Mastery framework. It begins with a particular working assumption that will drive our focus:

> The solution to a real problem preexists
> and will be found if we keep working
> the problem properly.

Mandalorian: *This is the way: When facing a real problem, it can be easy to feel overwhelmed and lost. But know this: the solution already exists, and it is waiting to be discovered. It is up to us to keep working the problem properly, to stay focused and committed,*

> *to trust in our better instincts and our ability to find the way forward. It may not be an easy path, but the solution is there, waiting to be found. So, do not give up, do not lose hope. Stay the course, and the solution will reveal itself to you in due time. This is the way.*

This may not sound like much at first glance. It may even seem obvious. But I promise you that thinking this way will make a world of difference to your life. It is a working assumption, perhaps a mental model, so we aren't exactly pretending it is absolutely true. Yet, we are believing it's a useful way to think. Let me clarify a few of the terms:

- A real problem is one that can be solved. Often, we spend time trying to fix something that is simply real. When we consider a complex problem like the climate, one of the elements is the sun. The sun is not something to fix, it's just an element of reality that we must consider. There is no solving the amount of heat the sun puts out. So, there is no sense in framing it as a problem. We might be able to do something about the sunshine. An umbrella, a cloud, or a tree can 'fix' the sunshine, but the sun itself isn't something to fix. Volcanic ash can certainly stop the sunlight and cool the earth, but we aren't going to fix the sun. You need to be aware of this because if you are trying to solve a reality, you are trying to solve an unsolvable problem. That turns out to be a big waste of time and energy. Additionally, the parts of the problem count too. If you have parts that are truly unchangeable, you

don't want to waste your time trying to problem-solve them.
- The thought that the solution pre-exists is vital. It keeps us looking for something that can be found. There is a famous story of G.B. Dantzig who was a mathematical scientist. In college, he showed up late for a class and saw statistical theory problems on the board that he assumed were homework. In a couple of days, he turned in the solutions with an apology for their lateness. It turned out that he solved problems that had been unsolved up until that point in time. By his own admission, he believed he would not have been able to solve them if he had known they were yet unsolved. There is power in the assumption that the solution pre-exists.
- Working the problem is often misunderstood. While working on it is useful, working on it to find an achievable goal is better. Of course, finding a goal that will solve the problem forever is glorious. Failure in anything is in the quitting. By definition, you haven't failed until you give up. Don't give up, just keep working the problem. As Fuller framed it,

You never change things by fighting the existing reality.
To change something, build a new model
that makes the existing model obsolete.
-Buckminster Fuller

If you'll trust me, use the process, and learn how to permanently solve your pressing problems, you'll be sold. In a way, I'm challenging you here to prove me wrong. If you really follow the process and find out how much better you become in attacking problems, you'll become an evangelist for enjoying problems and a hero to the people you help. Isn't that a legacy you'd like to embrace?

The Simple6 framework we've developed has a simple overall structure, remembered by six words:

SEEK * SEE * SORT * SIMPLIFY * SOLVE * SIMULATE

There are different ways you can work with this structure, but the pattern is still going to be the same. It is a sequence, to be followed in order. Honestly, it takes a little discipline to get good at this game of crafting solutions, but it is so worth it! The reason a little discipline is required is that we humans are not only given to guessing, but we are also given to intuitive leaps. Guesses and leaps are wrong more often than we dare admit. We can think a solution is awesome because, like magic, it came to us out of nowhere. That can happen, but good solutions can withstand being questioned. We have a variety of ways to apply this model, but we'll just focus on two of them: The Full Monty and Business Casual. In outthinking your problems, you'll want to learn to respect this sequence. Consider each:

1. **SEEK**: Seeking is the frame that dictates everything else in the Simple6 Model. Most models begin with problem definition, but that often gets us off course. Akin to the error in root cause analysis, if

you define the problem prematurely, you'll be off course. This first step sets the proper framework to understand why the problem exists. In this step, we are NOT asking, "What's the problem?" Instead, we ARE asking, "What do I want?" With teams in particular, there is nothing more unifying than and agreed upon answer to the question, "What do we want?" It is rarely asked, so each team member is covertly at odds with one another because their answers often vary. Here's the glaring reality that has been largely unnoticed throughout the history of formulating a universal problem-solving model:

> **There is no problem until somebody wants something.**
> -Fred Ray Lybrand Jr.

It's the desire that generates the problem. The common mistake is to attempt to define a problem when the desire is buried as an unconscious assumption. Assumptions are fine if you are lucky or intentional, but we are trying to rid problem-solving of luck and accidents (as much as possible).

2. **SEE**: Seeing is all about observation, about knowing what you are actually looking at. Humans do hallucinate a lot; they see things that aren't really there. "The magician really did saw that lady in half." "That video I saw on YouTube proves there are reptilians among us." "Your cat thinks you are amazing." But there is a solution to being tricked or missing something. We can observe without judging or making up a story to explain what we

see. In fact, the more you look, the more you see. It is vital to get good at looking at something with all the objectivity you can muster. Seeing is the foundation of crafting great solutions.

3. **SORT**: Sorting is about getting all the things we observed in step two into a variety of categories. Putting things into categories allows us to see even more, plus it gets us to see the emerging patterns we need for understanding the problem. For example, if you sorted the shoes in your closet into categories, they might look like this:

- Dress Up
- Casual
- Exercise
- Hard work
- Comfort inside

4. **SIMPLIFY**: Simplifying is perhaps the most profound part of the process. When we simplify, we are looking at the overall pattern of what's happening. It's really looking at the structure and the logic of how things are working (or not). Reading is a good example of the entire process up until this point. We can see the words and phrases, but then we must understand the categories. For example, each chapter of Dickens's A Christmas Carol is situated in different settings. The main character is at his office, then his house, then his

boarding school, etc. Finally, if we sort it all, we can see that it's about...

- A miserly man named Scrooge who is
- Visited by his dead business partner and
- Three spirits that show him

    a) His past,
    b) His present, and
    c) His future (if he doesn't change).

- Scrooge then realizes he has another chance because the future hasn't happened yet, and so he becomes the most generous man in town.

Understanding this flow of a book will allow you to remember and make sense of all the details. Simplifying is when you take all the things you sorted and put them into an easy-to-understand story. Insight comes when we are surprised by a switch to a better story. You might think the above is complicated, but notice I just explained a 30,000-word novella to you. It's a really handy trick in college too (show your kids)! Your problem has a story too and it may turn out just as well as Scrooge's did. Understanding the story is often the fast track to finding a solution.

Another way to simplify your understanding is to think about it in terms of an analogy or metaphor from day-to-day life. This can also help with explaining the solution to others. For example, if you have a problem with organizing things in a space, just think about a parking lot. You can let people just park wherever they want, but it will be pretty chaotic as it fills up. Unless, of course, you have painted lines in the parking lot. Painting lines, including sections for handicap parking and compact cars, maximizes the space. It allows the most cars to fit in an orderly way. I first heard this thought when someone explained formatting a hard drive in a computer. It's like drawing lines in the parking lot so all the information can be 'parked' efficiently. Wow, that made sense.

Simplifying the logic, structure, and story allows you to work effectively on a solution. The contrasting point is that you don't want to take refuge in complexity. The more complexity, the less you can see or sort, much less simplify and solve.

5. **SOLVE**: Solving is the process of coming up with a goal that will (ideally) make the problem go away forever. In this sense, it is the answer you need for the question you are asking. Of course, this makes the way we define the problem extremely important. Asking why you don't have more customers will lead to a lot of reasons or excuses. Asking, "How can I get more customers and keep them for life?" will take you in an entirely different direction. Remember, all goals are solutions to problems, at some level. Rollo May noticed that a great solution is often perceived as 'elegant'. It's true. When you

discover the right goal, that if reached, will make your problem go away eternally; it is elegant!

6. **SIMULATE**: The final move is Simulate. This step is already hidden in a question you'll learn to use in the solving step which asks, "Why would it work?" Nonetheless, it needs to be understood as a separate step in the process. Honestly, it is in play when we are in the solving stage since it is impossible to avoid implications when considering a goal that will permanently solve the problem. But, as a separate step, we are bringing wisdom to bear on the decision to pursue our solution. When we simulate a solution in our mind, we are building and running a model. The practice was on full display in the life of Nikola Tesla. Here's how this famous scientist described this technique:

> "I do not rush into actual work. When I get a new idea, I start at once building it up in my imagination and make improvements and operate the device in my mind. When I have gone so far as to embody everything in my invention, every possible improvement I can think of, and when I see no fault anywhere, I put into concrete form the final product of my brain."
> -Nikola Tesla

Obviously, Tesla is describing the use of his imagination throughout the whole process in creating a device. In the final moments, however, he is testing the machine to make sure it works.

You can do the same thing with a solution you've invented. Imagine it as something real and that is working.

- Why does it solve the problem?
- How does it solve it?
- What happens over time to other people or circumstances connected to the solution?

Playing this out in your mind can help you see potential problems created by the solution, if there are any. And it can also intensify your excitement and confidence in making the solution real. For the most part, if you can honestly imagine it really happening, then you probably have an answer that will work if you create it.

Now, you want to focus on the process itself. When you are ready, take a problem and run it through the Full Monty. First, however, read the next chapter to understand the process in greater detail. Using it will make you an exponentially better master of creating the solutions you need.

Here's a mundane example of a problem that plagued my mother for years. She often made us my favorite dessert, known as Fruit Cocktail Cake. The problem was that the cake almost always would 'fall' in the cooking process. Falling meant that it would collapse in the middle, but since the sauce was mostly sugar and butter, we loved that middle piece! Because she assumed that our being loud and stomping was the cause, she had us tiptoe through the house and whisper while it was in the oven. It worked occasionally enough to keep up the assumption. However, she finally discovered a flaw in her simple pattern. She was using baking soda instead of baking powder in her process. In this instance, it was a single step that was flawed. Had she checked it in the beginning by looking at her ingredients, the recipe, and the process, she would have solved the problem much earlier. Then again, it wasn't a problem for us as kids. We loved the cake as it was. Please take to heart that team building is very much the same as baking a cake that you've invented for those who will appreciate it. What are you missing that Seeking, Seeing, Sorting, Simplifying, Solving, and Simulating will help you overcome?

To be clear, we are not talking about what is commonly done with simulations and modeling as a predictive measure. Models are commonly used for weather, population growth, and resources depletion, etc. We aren't getting crazy or political here. We just want to make sure we've pondered how a solution might play out. There are two other words that we can use in the Simulation Step: Scenario and Score.

Scenario. Another way to simulate is to actively create scenarios, or scenes to look at how things might turn out. The simple way scenario is to create a Best Case, Worse Case, and Most Likely Case. If everything turns out perfect, what are all the great things that will happen and how smooth will the process go? That's the Best Case. If everything goes bad, as bad as you can imagine, what will happen? What could go wrong, really wrong? That's the Worse Case. Finally, what is the Most Likely Case? Given all you know, what is your best guess? It is always nested between the first two. If you pretend your likely and best-case scenarios are the same, you probably a seeing reality in the review!

Score. Another option is to score your solution. In other words, you can create a few parameters to measure the likelihood of success when your solution is implemented. For example, you could make a list of key factors (depending on the issue) such as cost, speed of implementation, number of people impacted, resistance from competitors or trolls, and personal bandwidth for focus. Next, assign each a score or grade and add them up. If your solution comes out to be a B-minus or 81/100, it might not really be the solution you are wanting. Also, this kind of scoring can help you target weaknesses. Ask, "Why did it get such a low score in a particular area?" Scoring is another way to simulate or evaluate the outcome a solution might create.

Final Note: There is a not-so-apparent reason Simulation is important in crafting solutions, and that is motivation. Even though humans need a goal to act, they can't move unless they are relatively confident about the plan. Simulation is a faith/hope building exercise that reduces questions and doubts below the level of resistance. Essentially, we are asking and answering the question, "Will this work?" While we can't know for sure, having some confidence we are on to a solution because we've thought it through and tested it a fair bit, is golden for motivation. Simulation must not be undervalued, but it must not be over-thought either. Work it through enough to where if I asked you, "Are you ready to take action right now?" you'd be able to quickly say, "Yes!" That should do it.

Business Casual and the Full Monty

In later chapters we will detail and use two approaches to solution creation. For now, just survey the approaches and see what they are pointing at. Of course, Solutions-Crafting is always pointing at a goal that will solve the problem eternally (if possible). The Full Monty is a British slang of unclear origins. It basically means things like 'the whole hog', 'the whole nine yards', or 'the whole shebang'. It has come to mean fully unclothed (thanks to Monty Python and a movie by the title). While the pop-culture version still matches, we are thinking about being fully clothed. One of the theories of origin is that the Full Monty had to do with a full set of clothes (vest included). When we say the Full Monty, we mean the whole process for crafting solutions. Business Casual, following the analogy, means a 'dressed down' version that is still quite helpful when you need some simplicity or speed. As with any process, there can be numerous subprocesses explored or added. Please don't worry about that just now. Aim to grasp the overall shape and flow, the 'how it works' in creating solutions.

Business Casual

Would you like to start with a quick success? Pick a problem and get to work. There are two versions of **The Simple6 Problem-Solving Model** that we will share here. If you find yourself without much time, or you are dealing with a personal problem, this shorter approach is a great way to go. We call it Business Casual. We'll walk you through it in Part III, but for now just get the idea alive in your mind. This is the short version we use all the time, especially with personal and less complex problems. It's especially helpful if you don't have much time and want to look for a solution with great efficiency. It is a fast version using SEEK, SEE, SIMPLIFY, and SOLVE. The Full Monty is about thoroughness and is especially valuable for teams and more complex, long-term, problems. Here are the key steps in the form of questions for Business Casual:

1. What do you think is the problem?
    a) Why is that a problem?
    b) Why is that a problem?

2. What do you want to happen?
    a) Why that?
    b) Why that?
    c) What happens if you win here?
    d) How would you now define the real problem?

3. What goal, if accomplished, would solve this problem forever?
   a) Why would it work?

4. How can the goal be reached?
   a) What are the major steps necessary for reaching the goal?
   b) What's the next step?
   c) When will you promise to complete the next step by?

Yep, that's all there is to it. Remember, the aim is to clarify the problem and look for a goal that is (if possible) a permanent solution. What are your top three pressing problems? Pick one and walk through these questions on paper. Playing with it first on paper will get you on course to the solution you've been needing all along. I'm going to show you how this works in a moment, but for now, give it a try and watch the magic begin! You will notice that we use the question 'Why?' a few times. The question 'Why?' helps you dig deeper. What do you think is the problem? The problem is that I don't have enough time. Why is not having enough time a problem? Because then I could get everything done that needs doing. Why does everything need to be done? Because we will fail if it isn't all done. So, how would you define the problem now? Everything needs to be done. Notice, how you would solve getting everything done will take you on a different course than trying to find out how to get yourself to have more time. You can use as many 'Why?' questions as you want to dig deeper.

The advanced framework for Solutions-Crafting is the Full Monty. I never saw the movie, but I know it means a full view! That's the idea. This is the full view, frontal and exposed, of how to craft the best solutions you can.

THE FULL MONTY

Here are the specific steps in our framework as a series of strategic questions:

SEEK

1. What do you think the problem is right now?
2. What are you most afraid of if this problem wins?
   a) Why is that a problem?
   b) Why else?

3. What do you want to happen?
   a) Why that?
   b) Why that?
   c) What happens if you win here?

4. How would you now define the real problem given what you want?

SEE

5. What are the relevant pieces or elements?
6. What else do you see that might relate?
   a) What else?
   b) Is the problem, or any of its elements unchangeable realities?

SORT

7. How would you sort the pieces into appropriate categories or groups?

SIMPLIFY

8. What is the flow, the logic, of how it all works?

SOLVE

9. What goal, if reached, would solve the problem forever?
   a) Why would it solve it?
   b) What else might work?
   c) Why would that solve it?
   d) What's the better goal?

10. How can the goal be reached?
    a) What are the possible paths?
    b) What would be a good organizing metaphor?
    c) What are the logical steps to reach the goal?
    d) What would you guess is the probability of success if you follow your plans?

SIMULATE

11. Check: Is there a good chance this is just a Reality that can't be solved? If yes, then are you attacking the wrong problem?

12. Imagine the solution being fully implemented and working at full capacity. What happens? What's good? What accidentally happens that is bad?
13. What is the Best-Case Scenario? The Worse-Case Scenario? The Most Likely Scenario?
14. What five factors would make a good Score Card? What grade would you give each area on how well the goal will solve the problem? What overall grade would you give the goal?

Chapter 7 Takeaways

- There is power in the assumption that the solution pre-exists.
- If you keep working the problem correctly, you'll find the solution eventually.
- The Simple6 moves in crafting solutions are SEEK, SEE, SORT, SIMPLIFY, SOLVE, and SIMULATE.
- Following a process increases your odds of success exponentially.
- Don't take refuge in complexity.
- Solving is the process of coming up with a goal that will (ideally) make the problem go away forever.
- The Full Monty and Business Casual are the two processes we offer to guide you through the SEEK, SEE, SORT, SIMPLIFY, SOLVE, and SIMULATE moves.

Chapter 8

Solutions-Crafting with The Full Monty

The purpose of this chapter is to explain our process and why all the elements matter in our framework. We introduced you to the Full Monty in the last chapter, but now it's time to explain it in detail. **The Full Monty is our comprehensive process for creating solutions that last.**

> **Mandalorian:** *This is the way: The purpose of this chapter is to take you deeper into our process, to give you a closer look at the elements that make up our framework, and to show you why each one matters. You may recall that in the last chapter, we introduced you to the Full Monty, the ultimate approach to crafting solutions that endure. Now, it is time to go Full Monty and delve into the nitty-gritty details of this comprehensive process. We will leave no stone*

unturned, no element unexplained, as we guide you through each step of the Full Monty. By the end of this chapter, you will have a full understanding of our approach, and you will be ready to start tackling any problem that comes your way. This is the way.

Understanding the 'how' behind the 'what' is very important. A lot of this happens intuitively. But, as in any sport, an athlete who is conscious of what they are doing has a great advantage over the competition. Each step is critical. But, as we explained with Business Casual, you are going to already be ahead of the game, even if you aren't an expert yet. Let's look at each component and why it is so valuable.

SEEK

1. **What do you think the problem is right now?**

    We begin with what you think about the problem. Here we are aiming for your best guess. There are a couple of reasons this is important. First, you probably are not defining the problem correctly. Usually, we are looking at the pain-point or the symptoms the problem is causing. This rarely gets us to the solution we need. But, getting that out in the open is important. Once we separate the symptom from the cause(s), we can begin to see with fresh eyes. What if you aren't putting out enough pizzas in your pizzeria? You can guess that the problem is that the team isn't working fast enough. Once that is out in the open you can think about getting them to work faster, how to cause that result. But, as you work the problem, you can also discover that your ovens can only cook 25 pizzas an hour (where you need 50). The bottleneck is your oven, not your employees. So, the problem definition will turn to the ovens, away from your employees. Second, when you express your guess about the problem, it establishes a way to evaluate the solution you discover later. If the solution doesn't take care of your initial guess at the problem, it's not the solution you want.

Both of these come together in defining a problem. If you can look at your definition and then guess where that might lead you, you'll have a better way to look at what you are facing. If you were to think your relationship problem is the other person, then that would point to 'fixing' the other person. When you think that through and realize that 'fixing' them is not a viable end result, you'll be able to rethink your definition of the problem. If the problem is defined as yourself, then the solution will be about you. If you see the problem as the relationship itself (how you both interact), then the solution will probably involve both of you. As you can see, the definition itself is paramount.

2. **What are you most afraid of if this problem wins?**

   a) Why is that a problem?
   b) Why else?

We could have a conversation about fear that would take up a whole book. Basically, you need to realize that **totally fearless individuals are just fools. You better fear mistakes and missteps, that's the essence**

of wisdom. Identifying what you are afraid of if the problem wins gives insight into your own motivations and into what the implications are for losing. For example, if you have an advertising problem, your fear is that you are wasting money. Wasting money can drain your resources, but it's more likely that you want the advertising money to produce the sales you want. Immediately, you can see that the issue really is about knowing if the advertising is working. You don't want to be like John Wanamaker who said, "Half the money I spend on advertising is wasted; the trouble is I don't know which half." With this insight, you'll naturally start looking at how to keep score, so the advertising problem won't win. Insisting that your solution shows a measurable result comes straight out of thinking through the implications. You want to win. You want your problem to exit the building.

3. **What do you want?**

   a) Why that?
   b) Why that?
   c) What happens if you win here?
   d) What do you really want?

One of the original insights of our framework is that we understand a profound truth:

> **There is no problem, in heaven or on earth, until somebody wants something.**
> -Fred Ray Lybrand

Finding out what you really want allows you to target the solution accurately. Often what we want is hidden behind the symptoms or pain-point that is screaming the loudest. A common example is how people often eat cereal with milk because they are thirsty, not hungry. Drinking a glass of water is all you might need, but not being clear on what you want drives you to a different solution. Think about what winning really looks like for you on this issue. Be honest, "What do you really want?"

4. **How would you now define the real problem given what you want?**

    In this step you are simply trying to articulate the problem in terms of what is wanted. This is commonly different from your first guess. The reason you want to write it down in a good form is so that your mind will stay on target. If you have a team, it's even more important to keep everyone focused on the same definition. Earlier, I explained the shift from the problem being a 'stuck pig' (oil pipeline issue) to creating '100% flow'. Throughout the division and among the teams, everyone was fluent and focused on creating 100% flow. That made everything clearer and smoother, it always does.

SEE

5. **What are all of the relevant pieces?**

    In this step you are trying to get all the elements involved identified. In a way, you are a mad scientist who is mixing chemical compounds. All the elements on the periodic table can be arranged in different ways to produce different things. Hydrogen and oxygen are combined to make H_2O, or water. Hydrogen, sulfur, and oxygen are combined to make H_2SO_4, or sulfuric acid. Your problem is a combination of elements, and once you know them, then you can be on the way to a different combination of elements or an altogether different solution. Honestly, this is an important skill to develop, but identifying any of the elements is usually a help. If you have a service business that interacts with the customer in their home, then you can see that you have the customer, the house, the thing in the house to do, the words of the customer, the words of your service person, and the time of day. There are more, but once you know even these pieces, you can begin to make sense of where the problem lives.

6. **What else do you see that might relate?**

   a) What else?
   b) Is the problem, or any of its elements, unchangeable realities?

The basic principle of observation is that the more you look, the more you'll see. Keep at it for a while. Keep clarifying your understanding and awareness of the relevant pieces. The more you grasp the parts of the problem, the better your ability to craft a solution. At this point, it is important to also admit which of these elements are unchangeable realities. In other words, if an element is essentially a fact (like the sun as an element of the temperature of the earth), then you won't be tempted to try to make it a changeable part of the solution. A lot of time is wasted trying to change unchangeable things. Of course, don't give up too quickly. At one point, all of the experts said the four-minute-mile was physically impossible for humans! Question 9 makes sure you think about this again in the solving step.

SORT

7. **How would you sort the pieces into appropriate categories or groups?**

   Putting them into categories that make sense also helps. In the pizza example, you basically have people, materials, equipment, and time. Getting the people to agree about the time and what is going to happen with the materials allows you to target your solution. Then again, there is a little more to it as you'll read below. There are no 'right' categories, but it is valuable to sort them in a variety of ways. This way of looking for a pattern can dramatically help you in the process of crafting your solution.

SIMPLIFY

8. **What is the flow, the logic, of how it all works?**

   Once you have the elements organized into categories, you can look at the logic, the sequence, the flow of what's going on concerning your problem. This is a look at the underlying structure that is giving rise to the results you are seeing, but don't want. In other words, things work in order. When things don't work, then either the order is dysfunctional or one or more of the elements are flawed (or are interacting in a flawed way). In the example above, we might see that it moves from person to materials to time to person to materials. Imagine you are paying someone to fix a hole in your wall. You call (person) and tell them you need to repair a hole in your wall (materials), then they set a time to arrive (time). You greet them when they arrive (person) and show them the hole in the wall (materials). This kind of exercise may seem a little tedious, but it is magical. It's just like when you do a jigsaw puzzle, getting the pieces organized by colors or sides or key lines. That act of organizing the pieces allows you to move along to solve the puzzle. It sets you up to have an approach to solving the puzzle that follows a logic, a flow. This approach is far more effective than randomly trying different pieces. **Most popular creative problem-solving approaches are more random, and more ineffective, than we realize.** You can get as sophisticated as you need to at this stage by using logic-trees, flowcharts, etc. Of course, the goal is to simplify things, so that engineer-style analysis can easily get in the way

SOLVE

9. **What goal, if reached, would solve the problem forever?**

    a) Why would it work?
    b) What else might work?
    c) Why would that solve it?
    d) What's the better goal?

Now you are ready to solve the problem. While we have addressed this already, let's think about it in a little more depth. A goal is an outcome or a result. It is a point of focus. People often try to get motivated by goals, but it's really what the goal will do for you that sets you in motion. Creators commonly create because they simply love the thing enough to create it, but it still solves the problem of the artist's longing heart. Do you have money goals? Health goals? Relationship goals? What about your leadership? All of these areas may have a goal of some kind, but reaching the goal will solve some problem or set of problems. If you change your approach to food and add exercise, you could see your weight get into a normal range. What does a good weight solve? Clothes will fit, blood pressure will drop, diabetes will be avoided, sleep apnea will diminish, and energy will go up. A lot of problems go away with that goal. Of course, it's not just that you want to make your object of focus a solutions-creating goal, you want to approach finding that solution in the best way possible. Thinking about a goal that will solve the problem eternally takes your thinking to a different level.

One of the more common challenges a business can have is pay raises and bonuses. I've almost never coached a leader that didn't wrestle with this one. Why? Well, it's because they are considering so many factors and are deciding on each person in some sporadic manner. Jim asks for a raise, and it's run up the flagpole for a yes or no. When I've helped a company standardize raises and bonuses with a process, it gets simple and mechanical. We give raises in this way and at this point. We give bonuses based on this number at this point. Coming up with a solution becomes much easier when it is asked with, "How could we give raises and bonuses so we never have to have a conversation about them with anyone?" Or "How can we set up a permanent system that automatically takes care of pay scales and bonuses?" Perhaps you keep a special bonus in reserve for outstanding work, but also have a system that makes sense to everyone (and is occasionally adjusted) as a permanent solution. In many ways, you just want to embrace your inner sluggard. When you are smart and lazy, you'll come up with ways to not have to do the same things over-and-over again. That's the essence of looking for goals that can become eternal solutions.

One Important Point: Please do not make your solutions or goals into 'don't wants'. It will never work well for you. When you don't want something, you create a picture of its absence. That's back to problem-soothing. Picturing something not being there is like seeing an invisible ghost. Or it might be like the old riddle of how a blank sheet of paper is that of a cow eating grass. Where's the grass? The cow ate it. Where's the cow? The cow left because there was no more grass.

You really are wanting to create a picture of the end result you desire, the goal that will solve the problem by default if it's achieved. You want to picture your team succeeding, your child being helpful, and your drive landing safely in the fairway. You don't want to try and picture your team not failing, your child not whining, and your drive not going in the lake. Those kinds of pictures aren't helpful for focus or planning. Don't want 'don't-wants' when it comes to creating solutions. You can start with a 'don't want' in describing the problem, but it is a fatal flaw to end there. And you will.

Finally, we do want to ask, "Why would that solve it?" The purpose of this question is to get ourselves to think through the mechanics and impact of the goal as a solution. If it makes sense, it makes sense. However, we also want to notice any unintended consequences. If you have a German Shepherd that barks too much and you decide on the goal of having his voice-box removed, it certainly solves the barking problem permanently. Yet, thinking through why it would work could quickly help you to think about what will happen without his voice-box. In this case, he couldn't bark at prowlers or with happy sounds when you come back home. Asking, "Why would that solve it?" is more completely explored in the last Simple6 step, Simulate (Questions 11-14). Nonetheless, it is valuable to start considering it as a working solution at this point in the process.

10. **How can the goal be reached?**

   a) What are the possible paths?
   b) What would be a good organizing metaphor?
   c) What are the logical steps to reach the goal?
   d) What would you guess is the probability of success if you follow your plans?

   In this step we are looking at planning. Having a plan is also a way to focus your motivation. In order to have total focus on a goal that will solve your problem, you'll need to know four things:

   1. A goal
   2. Knowing current reality
   3. A deadline
   4. A plan.

   When someone doesn't know how to get to where they want to go, they can't really get started. Looking at a variety of paths will allow you to pick the one that makes the most sense for your situation. The steps in the plan should be logical, which means that they'll make sense. If you follow these steps, will you likely arrive at the result you want? **A plan puts the odds in your favor.**

   The metaphor can also be an important part of the planning process. In some of our training, we like to get our clients to think like an artist. How would an artist solve this problem? A metaphor can be powerful. Think about growing your business like a crop grows. There is preparing the soil with plowing and fertilizing. Seeds or small plants are placed in the ground and nurtured. Water, weed, and pest-management are added until the plants are mature. Finally, the crop is harvested. If those are pictured as the phases of your business, you have a simple way to think about the plan. There is preparation, beginning, growth, and stability in view. Of course, another metaphor may work better for you. Play around with it and think about how your business is like a vacation, flight to the moon, sailing a boat, playing the Settlers of Catan, or anything you can think of. How is it like the metaphor? How is it different? A metaphor can be a shortcut to reminding yourself what you are doing, as well as leading the team that works for you.

Thinking about the odds of success will help you grow your confidence in the plan. If you have a logical plan that makes sense, but you think there is only a 2% chance of success, then something is wrong. When a plan is good, you can imagine it working. Of course, I'm not saying it will be easy, but I am saying it is doable. Make sure you think the odds are good for success. If they are not, keep working.

SIMULATE

11. **Check: Is there a good chance this is just a reality that cannot be solved? If yes, then are you attacking the wrong problem?**

Finally, we get back to the definition of the problem as a doublecheck. Sometimes we work through the process and discover that we are trying to change a reality. Remember, realities by their nature cannot be solved. When word processing and desktop publishing with computers became the standard way to create documents, typewriters went out of style (IBM, the dominant force, sold its typewriter division in 1991). Even though there is a nostalgic 'boom' for them, trying to figure out how to become a multi-million-dollar business by selling and repairing typewriters is not a goal that will solve a problem. Even good typewriters do not solve a problem in the business world, they are just a reality. The end of the typewriter is a reality, probably just like landlines will be someday. **Problems, by their nature, are solvable.** A reality is not solvable, it's just an element to factor in if it is relevant.

12. **Imagine the solution being fully implemented and working at full capacity. What happens? What's good? What accidentally happens that is bad?**

    Yes, like Tesla, play out the solution in your mind. There is no need for perfection here, but just think about how it would go. Happily see all of the parts working smoothly, producing the result you want. Then, imagine something that unexpectedly comes from the process. Who might be harmed? What byproduct might create a problem? Thinking this through helps you refine your solution and will often save you a lot of time and money.

13. **What is the Best-Case Scenario? The Worse-Case Scenario? The Most-Likely Scenario?**

    Go wild here but be truthful too. If it works without a flaw, what will happen? If it sort of works, but doesn't completely solve the problem, what would that be like? In between those two, is the Most Likely Scenario. Things tend to not be as bad or as good as we can imagine. Use this practice to help you tweak your solution and build your confidence with the odds. One side benefit of this process is that it will create an excellent way for you to communicate with a team or potential investors.

14. **What five factors would make a good Score Card? What grade would you give each area on how well the goal will solve the problem? What overall grade would you give the goal?**

    This is extra credit. Your issue may not need this level of reflection, but it remains a great exercise regardless. Thinking through five ways you would grade how well the goal will solve the problem adds a great deal of clarity. Not unlike giving a report card to a child's parents, it is a fair indicator of progress in getting educated. Straight A's is awesome, but it is also good to know that they child is falling behind in math. Your solution can be graded too. It's not for pressure or punishment, but to grow your confidence as you tweak the solution toward success.

Conclusion

I want to end this chapter by emphasizing an important myth for you to dismiss from your life as a leader. We are not all equally creative. Children are not more creative than adults. Brainstorming solutions is commonly a terrible way to problem-solve. Maybe I'm in trouble here, but I really want you to optimize your own skill by avoiding these unicorn burps. They are all connected to the same thing, the imagination. Some myth grew into an epic tale where a muse or a happy accident gave birth to a great idea. I guess that could happen, but when you really study the history of invention it is the history of hard work and better methods. So, bear with me for a moment as I get the rainbows out of the air.

Creativity is not universal. When you look at the math and define creativity properly, you'll find that it roughly follows a bell curve. Some people simply have a better knack for generating 10 uses of a brick or are loaded with Openness to Experience (Big 5 Model of personality). It's the same with IQ. Sorry, we are not all geniuses. However, this isn't the end of the story because we can learn from others, work with others, or follow the methods others have invented.

Children are not more creative. Children do play and can be imaginative, but they aren't writing symphonies or designing cathedrals. Creativity really must be understood in terms of its usefulness or usability. A child can imagine different ways to use a brick, but it turns out there is not much to do with it. **To create**

means to 'bring into being'. When we are formulating solutions to our problems, we need real-world ideas that can come alive. I love children and enjoyed being a child myself, but they are learning to harness their imagination. They are not the ones to model our creativity after. Creating like a child in problem-solving most commonly sounds like crazy thoughts.

Brainstorming isn't the place to start. Brainstorming drifted from Alex Osborne's original idea. Today, brainstorming is largely a non-judgmental approach to just getting everyone to throw out into the room any ideas. There are two problems with this technique. First, it is often undirected. There isn't a clear idea of what the group is trying to solve for, how the problem is defined. Throwing out ideas that are undirected can simply lead to a lot of confusion and misdirection. Second, this caters to thinking we are creative kids. Having a new engineer throw out ideas for a seasoned engineering problem is rarely helpful (and they don't want to talk anyway because they are new). Once there is a frame on the problem, brainstorming with the right people can be great. Osborne took that approach, and we can too.

Finally, what we do know is that **if you follow a method consistently, you will see consistent results.** This is as true of creativity in solution-creation as it is in following a recipe. It's rather amazing that we can follow a recipe for an award-winning dish and see it come out close to the chef's original invention. This is what we are sharing with you here, a form for Solutions-Crafting, creating the results you want that remove the problems you don't.

Chapter 8 Takeaways

- The Full Monty is our comprehensive process for creating solutions that last.
- Every part of the Full Monty process matters.
- Your first guess at defining the problem is probably wrong, but it's important to get it out in the open.
- If the solution doesn't take care of your initial guess at the problem, it's not the solution you want.
- There is no problem, in heaven or on earth, until somebody wants something.
- Creativity is not universal. We all are not equally creative.
- Brainstorming is not the place to start, but defining the problem correctly is.
- If you follow a method consistently, you will see consistent results.

PART III

Chapter 9

Solutions-Crafting Step 1: Outthink Your Anxiety

There's a good chance you turned here first, which is awesome. If you've jumped into this book and started here, that's great, and welcome! However, the preceding chapters laid the groundwork for this chapter, so I recommend you read all of them first. However, if you want to start here, that's ok with me. Let's outthink your anxiety.

> **Mandalorian:** *This is the way: It is good to see you here, and I welcome you with open arms. You may have arrived at this chapter first, which is admirable, but the previous chapters have set the foundation for what is to come. Therefore, I suggest that you read them before diving into this one. However, if you are ready to take the plunge and start here, I will not stand in your way. Let us focus on the task at hand*

> and outthink the anxiety that may be holding you back. Together, we will forge a path to overcome any obstacle that comes our way. This is the way.

First, realize **anxiety can be good.** Yes, it's true. All emotions are good when you learn what they are trying to tell you, and how to direct them. **Anxiety leads to a wonderful feeling when the anxiety ends.** Think of great suspenseful movies, football games, or rollercoaster rides. Isn't it exhilarating when the ride is over and you survived (or prevailed)? Of course it is. Anxiety is a way to rev up your body and focus your attention. The last thing we need is a brain surgeon, or an explosive ordnance disposal specialist, to be too relaxed! Your anxiety can tell you that something matters, that you should bring your A-game to the moment. Anxiety is not dysfunctional by itself; it's just trying to tell you to pay attention.

Second, you are not alone. **Every leader must learn to master their anxiety.** It's exciting to start a new enterprise, but if you are not somewhat terrified, you simply don't understand the game you're playing. You are a human being and there is risk and reward ahead. Worse yet, your spouse, friend, significant other (and maybe your pet) may also be anxious because they are in the life-raft with you! Hey, be stressed, but relax. You are totes normal, except for the part where you think you can beat the odds and build an amazing future. What if you fail? Well, every leader thinks that it is worth the price of admission. If there isn't a rollercoaster, you are probably at the wrong amusement park.

Third, **outthinking your anxiety is the lever for overcoming your pressing problem.** Though we've mentioned it before, I want you to really embrace why you can't solve problems when you are too anxious. The simple reason is that you are not an idiot, you are not self-destructive, you are not a fool. If you are a fool, then nothing you read can save you. You have the wrong friends, the wrong coach, and the wrong way to think. Your foolishness will catch up with you because you are simply not afraid of the right things. Fools do not fear the right things. Good luck. If you are still reading, then I bet you are not an idiot because you are teachable. Teachability is about being willing to unlearn in order to learn. If you can't see that you're wrong, you'll never be able to see how to get to right. Think about something like sales. If you are too anxious to pitch your offer to someone, then you never will. Anxiety is trying to protect you from harm. If working on a problem is seen as harmful, then how can you even think about it? The key is to be anxious about real things and not imaginary ones. That's what we are getting at. Be afraid, but don't stay afraid of a nightmare that is just a bad movie you're watching while you are asleep. The super-majority of your stress is built on something imaginary; I promise. Let's get into reality, or get reality into you, and make your anxiety melt away. Ready?

Why is erasing our anxiety so hard? Why is it such a challenge? **More than anything, it is our lack of understanding how anxiety works that makes dealing with it so difficult.** Human beings have instincts, but not many. Almost everything has to be learned by humans, compared to animals. But some things we can do without being taught. There is a movie from 1991 called *Little Man Tate*. In it they defined a genius as one who "...learns without studying and knows without learning. That he is eloquent without preparation, exact without calculation, and profound without reflection." If that's true, it's the exception of genius, not the rule for the rest of us. The remaining 99.9% of us must learn by studying, know nothing without learning, must prepare, calculate, and reflect a lot. We don't really know much of anything without learning how and what and why. Even Mozart had to learn the musical scale. I'm telling you this because dealing with anxiety is not an instinct. You can't just 'common sense' your way out of anxiety. We may be instinctively afraid, but we can overcome our fear by learning how to think better.

So, what do you need to know about anxiety? How does it work? There are a variety of things that might cause anxiety in terms of neurochemistry and personality (see Neuroticism in the Big Five traits). If you have ongoing anxiety that isn't dependent on a situation or circumstance, or that is overwhelming your life, please seek professional help. However, there are things you can learn to run your emotions, specifically in erasing the anxiety common to leaders. Let's think about it.

To start, you must realize that anxiety is about the future, while depression is about the past. You can't be anxious about the past because it has already happened, it's done. Fear is about what is ahead, and specifically what is bad about what is ahead. Anxiety is about anticipating a worse future. Clearly this is unique to you, so it is a future you do not want to happen. We can see the individual nature of this problem by noticing that the same event is seen differently by different people. Every weekend we see this in sports.

Fans are for one team or player to win against the other team or player. You cheer for your team and feel bad when they lose. On the other hand, if the other team beats your team, they are happy. It's the same event, one team won. There are different experiences based on one's interpretation of the event. Anxiety is the lead-up to the anticipated defeat. What is ahead that you think is going to be worse for you than what's happening right now?

Next, it is important to realize that when you are anxious, you aren't just thinking about negative possibilities, you believe them. You have faith that a bad thing is going to happen. If you are stressed about something in the future, I can assure you that you are a person of great faith. The problem with faith is that we can direct it toward the wrong thing. This is where we get 'Doubting Thomas', who actually had the faith to say about Jesus, '"Let's also go, so that we may die with Him!" He knew things would be bad, though it turned out that they didn't die with Him. Thomas wasn't anxious, however. Anxiety mixes in a slight amount of hope with faith. We believe a bad thing will happen, but we have some hope that it might not. It's as though we 'know' it's going to happen and be bad. But we also 'don't know' for absolute sure. When you know for absolute sure that a bad thing will happen, you become hopeless and resigned to the outcome. That's what Thomas was doing above. When we conclude that something we don't want is guaranteed to happen, we treat it like a past event in our minds. It has sort of 'already happened', so we feel sad, depressed, or despondent. It's like hope. If you know something has happened, you can't really hope that it won't. When you don't know, but believe, an unwanted thing will happen, you will be anxious. The moment it happens, the anxiety is replaced by disappointment. As mentioned above, if you stay with something bad in your past long enough, you can turn it into regret and depression.

Finally, you must understand that anxiety dismisses all other possibilities. It's a focusing mechanism, as if your anxiety wants to stay alive and have no competition. We commonly think that the only thing we have to fear is fear itself, but this is quite off the mark. We don't fear the unknown. If you knew you would die in your car today, we would not be able to force you into the car and drive. However, you could die in your car today anyway. You really don't know, so you wear a seatbelt, drive safely, and stay away from dangerous drivers. Anxiety only focuses on one possibility. You can't have faith if you don't really 'know' how things will go. Faith is about drawing a conclusion, so in this sense it is a settled issue in your mind. You are anxious because you 'know' the bad thing is going to happen. This kind of 'knowing' isn't 100%, but it has ruled out the other options, so you are anticipating the bad thing happening. Imagine you hate cold and are going to jump in the icy water at the Coney Island Polar Bear Plunge. Wouldn't you 'know' it's going to hurt at first, so you will anticipate the pain that's coming? If you have something in your situation that you anticipate being bad, then you will experience anxiety. That's basically how it works. So, in review we can see: Anxiety is about the bad future you don't want.

1. Anxiety is about the bad future you don't want.
2. Anxiety is hoping not, but believing that, the bad future you don't want will happen.

3. Anxiety dismisses all other possibilities.

In other words, anxiety is all in your thinking. Anxiety is guessing with confidence. If it turns out that the thing doesn't happen, then your anxiety was completely unnecessary. Already, this points to a solution, but let's run it through our Business Casual framework first before we look at how to outthink our anxiety.

1. What do you think is the problem?

    a) Why?
    b) Why?

A first guess about the problem would be that a particularly bad thing is going to happen. They are going to call my loan, I'm going to lose my major customer, or my best employee is going to leave for a better salary, etc. The problem is that the thing is going to happen. But where does that lead? So, we ask, "Why?" again. It's a problem because I must have the loan, customer, or employee, etc. Why? Without my loan, customer, or employee, my business will fail. So, the problem is that your business is going to fail. It may seem like this is a bit of a 'duh', but it is not. It gets us the underlying source of the anxiety. It's the same with teams.

2. What do you want to happen?

    a) Why do you want that?
    b) Why do you want that?
    c) How would you now define the real problem?

I want my team to succeed. Why? I want it to grow and provide good things for my shareholders/ bosses/ customers, and good things for my family and employees. Why? Because it's why I got into this enterprise and success is the best way to make all of this happen

3. **What goal, if accomplished, would solve this problem forever?**

The goal really is to establish a viable and prosperous company that has a good strategy which produces the money needed, has happy customers, and happy employees. So, depending on which of those is at risk, I need a customer, employee, or money goal that will work well 'forever'.

4. **How can the goal be reached?**

The goal can be reached with a further part of the process that could also reduce anxiety, but for now we'll stick with the first three questions. Though the above is a fair run at it, I realize it is hypothetical. I can do this with some ease because I'm not the one in the middle of it. There are two ways to outthink anxiety:

a) Outthink the imaginary basis of the anxiety.
b) Solve the problem.

In our experience, it is incredibly difficult to think effectively about solving the problem if the imaginary basis of the anxiety is in play. First, outthink the anxiety. Second, solve the problem.

The following is one of many techniques for reducing anxiety that is intensified by imaginary thinking. Here is where you can learn to outthink your anxiety. Again, it comes down to faith. Remember, you have situational anxiety because you are 'sure' that one specific thing you don't want to happen is just ahead in the future. If you can generate two more plausible outcomes for the same event, then you can't be sure what will happen, and your 'faith' will collapse. Anxiety can't thrive when we know we don't know the future. In full disclosure, I have an earned doctorate in Applied Theology. I only tell you this because the solution is born from theology/philosophy and not from psychology. This isn't psychobabble, though it is psychologically sound. As they say, "You can doubt anything if you question it enough." If you work with this technique, you will see your anxiety diminish. As it diminishes, you can then work more creatively on crafting a solution that will last.

DR. FRED'S HANDY-DANDY ANXIETY OUTTHINKER CHECKLIST (TO BE PRACTICED)

- How anxious do I feel? [1-10 scale]
- Do I clearly know what I feel anxious about happening in the future? What's the story?
- Am I anxious or just excited (or a little of both)? Assume 'excitement' when possible. It's often hard to distinguish between the two.
- Is what I'm actually anxious about happening now in real time? Really?
- Do I really think I know the future?
    - Am I a prophet or prophetess?
    - What 2 or 3 other stories could possibly happen?
    - Are my hopes of good things happening in the future clear in my mind?
        - What do I want?
        - What will it feel like if what I want happens?
        - Can I easily picture this story of what I want?
    - Do I now notice my anxiety has lessened? [1-10 scale]

Let's think about a common example together. Since we know that people would rather die than give a speech (I work with people all the time on this one), let's begin there.

- How anxious do I feel? [1-10 scale]

    I feel pretty anxious, probably about a 7 or 8.

- Do I clearly know what I feel anxious about happening in the future? What's the story?

    I'm giving a short talk about my experience moving from a full-time job to a free-wheeling entrepreneur. I don't speak much and, when I do, I get out of breath because I think I'll probably just sound confused by bouncing around. I want to talk, but I also want to avoid hurting my brand by sounding like an idiot.

- Am I anxious or just excited (or a little of both)? Assume 'excitement' when possible. It's often hard to distinguish between the two.

    I am anxious, but I guess I'm also excited. This talk will let me get contacts for the business and connect me a little more to the community. So, that's exciting.

- Is what I'm actually anxious about happening now in real time? Really?

I'm trying to prepare the talk, so that makes me anxious. But really? No, I'm not giving the talk right now. I'm not in front of a crowd.

- Do I really think I know the future?
    - Am I a prophet or prophetess?
    - What 2 or 3 other stories could possibly happen?

I am not a prophet, so I clearly don't know the future. I dn't know if the talk will be good or bad.

Other Stories: Besides it going bad and me sounding like an idiot? it's possible that I could do a good job and people would be responsive and encouraging. It could be that I do an OK job and they think it is really good. I also guess people could be glad that they are not the one speaking, so they are cheering for me. I also could practice it enough with someone who could coach me, which would mean it would at least be OK.

- Are my hopes of good things happening in the future clear in my mind?
    - What do I want?
    - What will it feel like if what I want happens?
    - Can I easily picture this story of what I want?

I want them to get something useful from my talk. That's more important than liking me. If people tell me that what I shared was helpful it will feel great. I can picture people saying, "Thank you, that was really helpful." It's not a hi-def 4K picture, but I can see it happening.

- Do I now notice my anxiety has lessened? [1-10 scale]

Yes, my anxiety is like a 3 or a 4 now.

The real key to this process is to calm your imagination. If you are imagining that the event is happening now, you'll be anxious. If you imagine that you know the future, you'll be anxious. If you think only one thing can happen, and it's bad, you'll be anxious. **The key to the whole process is to generate at least two more options of what 'could' happen.** One might be more likely, but if you can admit that it can go different ways, then you really can't be 'sure' about your one option. Of course, when you are not sure about what will happen, there isn't a good way to be overly anxious about it.

Finally, please embrace this as a skill to master. You will get a lot of benefit just working though the Anxiety Outthinker Process, but it will only be an issue-by-issue tool. Having it in your tool chest is great, but making it an ongoing part of your life is transforming. The key is intentional practice. If you'll take 10 minutes every morning for just a week, you'll see serious progress. In 10 minutes, you can go through the checklist thoughtfully about three times on any problem that is causing stress and anxiety. In time, as you develop mastery, you'll have the interesting experience of noticing you are anxious and being surprised (because it's been so long). With your anxiety and stress subsiding, you are ready to really remove it completely by creating an eternal solution. Next chapter.

Chapter 9 Takeaways

- Anxiety can be good and often leads to a wonderful feeling when the anxiety ends.
- Every leader must learn to overcome their anxiety.
- Outthinking your anxiety is the lever for overcoming your pressing problem.
- Anxiety is about the bad future you don't want.
- Anxiety is guessing with confidence.
- The key is to generate at least two additional options of what 'could' happen.
- The Anxiety Outthinker checklist can help you learn the skill of ending your anxiety.

Chapter 10

Solutions-Crafting Step 2: Discover Your Solution

What you really need is to solve your problem by creating a solution. Marsh Fisher, the co-founder of Century 21, got bored in retirement. So, he launched out to understand creativity. When he made sense of innovating new ideas, he got it down to an essential:

> The solution to any problem is just an idea.
> -Marsh Fisher

> **Mandalorian**: *This is the way: The path to victory lies not in solving problems, but in crafting solutions. To truly overcome the obstacles in your path, you must harness the power of your creativity and ingenuity. Instead of getting bogged down by the complexities of the problem, focus on envisioning a future where the*

> *problem is no longer a hindrance. With this mindset, you can unlock your potential and create a solution that not only solves the problem but propels you forward towards your goals. This is the way.*

One day I spent over an hour talking with Marsh at his invitation. I bought his Idea Fisher software, and it included the opportunity for Marsh to show you how to use it. We talked a lot about creativity, but only a little about the software. It was an awesome conversation. The most interesting thing he said was that it's shocking at how few people take him up on the offer to talk. I'm going to feel the same. Down the road you are going to have an opportunity to talk with me (or someone trained by me), but you probably want seize the opportunity. But really, that's not the problem. The problem is that you are going to know this material could change your leadership and the lives you'll impact. Next, you'll get busy, distracted, and perhaps chase the next 'new answer'. Hey, you've found the answer here. Stop and Act!

Review: The 5 Essentials About Problems

Let's highlight a few things here as we look to creating solutions.

First, problem-soothing is what most people do. They look at the point of pain, or symptom, and then brainstorm ways to make that go away. This approach is by far the most common way people are taught to problem-solve. It's a genuinely terrible approach because it all-but-guarantees seeing the same thing over-and-over again. If you can't meet a deadline, but scramble around with shortcuts or a refreshed promise, you can cover yourself this time. But, what about next time? What about the next after that? It's this kind of scrambling that eventually erodes team success. It is an entirely different world when you think about succeeding rather than not failing.

Next, your first guess probably doesn't define the problem properly. Most approaches to problem-solving get this right, but they don't realize what is causing the problem. Nonetheless, when you stop too soon and mis-define the problem, you are almost guaranteed to miss the solution. Even on the mundane level, if you think the problem is that the sidewalk is burning your feet, you won't come up with wearing shoes. Instead, you'll try to invent ways to cool the sidewalk or just give up and stay inside. Maybe we do want cooler sidewalks in Phoenix, but that's a different problem than your feet are burning.

Third, the problem is created by what you want. Being honest and clear about what you want is a necessary part of Solutions-Crafting. The moment you want something is the moment you have a problem to solve. If you want a new product to add to your offering, then the problem is figuring out what to offer. If you want it to be cutting edge, then that's one direction. If you want customers to desperately want it, then that's probably a different direction. Sometimes we want something we can't have, like wanting it to rain more in west Texas. It's not going to rain more than it does, so being in touch with that allows you to think in a better way for your ranch. Wanting to get and store water is something you might accomplish. Finding plants and animals that are low-water-needed can be a solution to how you use your land.

Fourth, a goal is always a solution to some problem or problems. It may be our temptation to worship an ideal, or it may be just reading the wrong stuff, but people commonly think goals are picked out from the ether because of a desire to create something we'd love to see. I'm sure you'd love to see anything you create, but the motive behind it invariably has some want-based problem in the background. You can prove this to yourself by picking a goal to think about and asking, "What problems does this solve if it happens?" You can also go back in time with the same plan. JFK set a goal of landing on the moon within a decade. What problems would that solve? The big one was to beat the Russians to the moon. America had lost getting the first man in orbit, so she could certainly win here. There is a lot more, likely including clandestine reasons we know nothing about, but it underscores the point. If you are a writer and want to write a book because you'd love to see it exist, then great. But aren't there problems underneath? You could be lovesick for the book. It could be a means of fame, money, opportunity, etc. It could just scratch your itch to create, but isn't an itch a problem? Leaders want all these things too, including just seeing if they can make it happen. It's about winning the leadership game, which in turn, is about overcoming the problem of losing the leadership game. Setting a goal that will solve the problem by default is the secret to focus and success.

Fifth, success is marked by a trail of solved problems. Whether in business or in relationships, solving problems forever is magical. Every situation has any number of problems that need to be addressed. Maybe it's your financials or your time-management or your hiring process. Bouncing back-and-forth between them can be exhausting. However, if you solved just one of them by a focused effort, a lot of energy would be freed up to tackle the next one. It's the same in a marriage, where the problems can involve roles, parenting, romance, finances, in-laws, communication, etc. Solving one of these issues forever (i.e. resolving the issue), gives momentum and energy to making real progress. It may seem impossible, but I assure you that you can solve a problem such that you'll never see it again. It's a matter of focus, which is not about concentration, but about coming back to the issue again-and-again until you win.

Now it's your turn. Get out a pad and pen and walk through these steps below. It's not that we want you to find an instant answer and quit reading, rather it's that we want you to experience how to start outthinking your problems. I can explain to you how to swim, but you need to get in the water to really learn. Now we can think about drawing up a solution using the shorter process. This is like a case-study, but it's with the imagination. I repeated the steps here for your convenience.

BUSINESS CASUAL EXERCISE

My Problem Title _____

1. What do you think is the problem?
   a. Why is that a problem?
   b. Why is that a problem?
2. What do you want to happen?
   a. Why that?
   b. Why that?
   c. What happens if you win here?
   d. How would you now define the real problem?
3. What goal, if accomplished, would solve this problem forever?
   a. Why would it work?
4. How can the goal be reached?
   a. What are the major steps necessary for reaching the goal?
   b. What's the next step?
   c. When will you promise to complete the next step by?

What you are going to see is the power of some 'aha' as an elegant solution appears. Often you make progress in just a few minutes. But it might take some time and effort. You might even have to sleep on it. But you will see things become clear and hopeful as you follow the steps. Moving from your guess about the problem, to getting it clear by examining what you want, and then settling on a goal that will focus your actions is magical. Coming back to it a few times just lets you see things with fresh eyes. Your brain is only working on the problem when you are focused on it, which is another reason you need to chillax your anxiety first. If you are too anxious, then there is no focus.

When you get down to it, you do want a picture in your head of the end result. Maybe you've hired the right person or put-up billboards in the area. You can also write it down, but in either case you are going to view it as a present reality. This picture you have of the result can grow and improve over time, but it is clearly something you will feel good about seeing as a finished product or event. If you don't feel good about it, then you aren't quite there. The good feeling is about motivation. Just as you feel bad about the likelihood of a problem happening, you also want to feel good about the problem going way. The goal will make the problem go away, so if you don't feel good about it something is amiss. Perhaps you don't think it's possible, or maybe your picture is just too vague. Draw it up in your mind and test it with your feelings. If you are not there, no problem; just keep working at it.

Chapter 10 Takeaways

- The solution to any problem is just an idea.
- The 5 Essentials About Problems
    1. Problem-soothing is what most people do.
    2. Your first guess probably doesn't define the problem properly.
    3. The problem is created by what you want.

4. A goal is always a solution to some problem or problems.
5. Success is marked by a trail of solved problems.

- If you are too anxious, then there is no focus.

- You want a picture in your head of the end result.

Chapter 11

Solutions-Crafting Step 3: Design Your Plan

You can call it what you'd like. But you need a plan, strategy, or path to get you from where you are (here) to where you want to go (there). There's really no way around it. Oftentimes we are stymied because we don't know what do next. Of course, that's what a plan is, it's knowing what to do next.

> **Mandalorian**: *This is the way. It is not enough to simply identify the problem. To truly outthink it, you must craft a solution that will lead you to your desired destination. This requires a plan, a strategy, a path. It is the way of the warrior to always have a plan, to always know what to do next. There is no plan when you do not know what to do next. So let us forge ahead*

and let us find the solution that will bring us victory. This is the way.

We'll go through the steps we've outlined in this book, but I want you to know the first principle:

The Next Step is Never Hard.

In the deeper training about solutions-crafting, I spent some time with Jennifer. Jennifer is a former assistant professor at Yale University. I shared this next step idea with her in our series of interviews. A few days after our discussion she told me she had been stuck. Her old tricks didn't help. But she said this one idea completely recovered her motivation and focus. Here's a part of the interview:

> ***Jennifer:*** *Well, you are a Solutions-Crafter. Do you have a solution crafted for getting in motion when we're stuck?*
>
> ***Dr. Fred:*** *You know, oddly enough I do. (Laughs) There is a way to get unstuck and I want to take time on this. This is an important sub-point of planning and implementation. To give people the opportunity to genuinely appreciate how getting things done happens, we want to know it works like this at the basic level:* ***The Next Step is Never hard.***
>
> ***Jennifer:*** *The next step is never hard. I was just pondering that, and it sounds like the opposite of what you're talking about. What does it mean and how does it work?*

Dr. Fred: *Yeah, the next step is never hard. I really want to help everyone understand something about human nature because if you get this principle down (that the next step is never hard), then you're in a position at any moment in time to make another step. Honestly, it's the old thing about a step where they say a trip of a thousand miles begins with one step. If you go out, just to a shopping area, a mall, the club, go wherever you want; just watch people for a little bit. Everything you see them do tells you the reason they're doing what they do. They think their next action is the easiest thing for them to do at that moment. That is the way it works. Human beings do what's easy, and I'm going to tell you they do what's easy because they're incredibly intelligent, not because they're lazy. The lazy people just think it's easier to be lazy, but you and I know there are people that work all the time. For them, it's easier to work all the time than to lay around. I'm kind of a little bit that way; the joke in my family is that relaxing stresses me out. (Laughs)*

Jennifer: *(Laughs)*

Dr. Fred: *When I'm on vacation, in about 3 or 4 days I'm telling my wife, "Oh how I'm wasting my life." What am I doing? I'm having to debrief and unwind. I've gotten a little better, but the fact is if you look at anything a person does, you'll see the truth. Look at how any person swings a golf club, the way they swing it is the easiest way for them to swing it to get their result. Their result may be crummy, but they are still swinging that way because it's easy (if only in their* mind). When you see someone getting an item off the shelf in a store, it's easier for them to get it than to ask for help. But sometimes it's not, and so they ask for help from someone with a ladder to come and get it. It's easier to ask for help than to climb the shelves! Every bit of behavior you see in human beings, whether children or adults, can safely take this into account. What's going on is that in the moment, from their viewpoint, their perception, their understanding, their situation, they are doing what is easiest to do. You know when people get married, it's easier to get married than to stay unmarried. You know something about their hopes and dreams. I'm not saying anything is bad or good here, I'm just saying it's true. When people quit a job, it's easier to go look for another job than to stay in that one. Furthermore, you can go down the list on how people spend their money, how they vote, even how they put a list together. We simply do what's easy or easier. Now if you understand that and spend some time just watching for it, you can also watch yourself. This is exactly what we all do. Now my statement that the next step is never hard actually can begin to make sense. I want to give an example—climbing a mountain. If you can imagine the mountain is not particularly high, but it's one of those mountains that has a sheer rock face. The elevation is up high enough to have a nice vista from which to look down on a beautiful valley. So, what you have is a little tourist stand that you can look down to the bottom of the sheer rock cliff. You can climb the sheer rock cliff, or there's a tourist trail that weaves up and around other little *vistas and platforms where you can stop. This trail continues all the way up to the main lookout point— the main vista there at the top of the mountain.*

You have the tourist stroll path, a little hike, or you have the rock-climbing path. Now if you think that through, you can understand that to make someone who wants to take the tourist path climb the rock wall would be very hard, even torturous; and yet oddly enough, if you know any rock climbers, for them to walk the tourist path just to 'be up there' would be torturous to them. Their motives are different, so it's easier for a rock climber to climb up the cliff than it is to walk up the trail. And it's easier for someone who just wants to see the view to walk up the trail, rather than it is to climb the sheer rock cliff. That's the nature of why the next step is never hard but this is what we get down to. When a person is walking on one of those little trails, every particular step, the next one, is easy. It's not hard at all, it's just a step and even when you come to a place you have to step up on the roots, you step up on that little root, and then take the next step. Each of those steps is easy, the same with rock climbing, their next step is just put my toe over into this little crevasse here you know, (Laughs) this little bump on the sheer rock face that could hold my toes or hold my shoe is nothing and then the next little step is easy too.

What happens to us if we try to jump several steps? That's what's hard. Imagine being in the wild and wanting to cross a ravine. You look at it and say, "I can't jump it, it's too far." But that's not the next step.

The next step is to jump down to that little ledge, then jump over to that narrow space under the other ledge, and then climb back up to the other side. The next step is never hard, the problem is we jump ahead.

The next step is never hard, which is incredible. If you get it and you look at what you're doing, but you think it's hard, that's not the next step. If you're going to implement a solution you've got and it looks hard, you're obviously not on the next step. The next step is never hard, and once you understand that, if it's easy then you'll find that you can do it.

Here is the summary, and it's all about making a workable plan to reach your goal, your solution:

The journey of 1,000 miles begins with putting on your sandals.

Well, there you have it. Planning is just putting together the path of steps, starting with the easiest! Here is the list we think is wise to consider as you create your plan to reach your goal:

1. How can the goal be reached?
   a) What are the possible paths?
   b) What would be a good organizing metaphor?
   c) What are the logical steps to reach the goal?
   d) What is the probability of success if you follow your plan?

Basically, a plan or strategy is a way to organize your actions so that it makes sense. Saving $100 a month to get to $50,000 in one year does not make sense. It's in the right direction, but the math/logic adds up to $1200, so it misses the mark. On the other hand, having a plan does not mean that you'll follow it exactly. In fact, no strategic plan has ever been followed exactly. There are always adjustments that need to be made. Nonetheless, it doesn't diminish the importance of the plan. If you have a treasure map and follow it, things are fine until you find out a mudslide wiped out the road years before. You certainly don't have to quit. Just figure out how to get back on the path. What's that chant? "Over, under, around, or through. Whatever it takes, that I'll do!" Well, maybe you're not a Marine or a Navy Seal, but having a plan does help you focus on what needs to be done.

Just think through possible paths. In fact, always try to come up with at least three ways to do it. One shortcut I like is the way Marsh Fisher looked for ideas based on association.

First, you get words that are related to your problem. Next, you list more words that are related to each of the words you listed. Finally, you ask, "How could this help me here?" for each of the words. For example, let's say I want a new snack product. Here's the first list:

Chip
Crunchy
Dip
Roll
Sauce

Next,

Chip.... Corn, Thin, Potato, Shape, Size
Crunchy
Dip
Roll
Sauce

Next (picking on Thin),

Thin...Thick, Long, Short, Stacked

Finally, how can 'thick' help me here? How can 'long' help me here? How can 'short' help me here? These questions, even from semi-random words allow us to 'fish' for ideas. As I ponder this, I notice that I love to find two corn chips that are stuck together. Why not intentionally create a batch of those bad-boys and call them 'Doubles', or something like that?

Well, that's not a planning example, but it is the same game. Often you can work backwards and see a good path, but creativity can kick in here for better options. When you work through the Full Monty, all of the elements will give you a good idea of the path to take. When you think about the logical steps, a metaphor, and the odds of success, it will come together for you.

If you want to add investors, you can look in several areas. Venture capitalists, family members, friends, and other leaders are all options. As you think it through, you might want to avoid venture folks and friends. However, thinking it through completely helps you know why and why not in your planning. Is it a loan or equity ownership you are selling? What will you guarantee? What will you not guarantee? This is not the place to bog down, but it is the place to think about your specific goal that will solve your specific problem if it's reached. Somewhere I heard Jordan Peterson mention that we should ask ourselves the following:

- Where am I?
- Where do I want to go?
- What's the least complicated way to get there?

Yes, that's what I've been saying for decades. The third point is the planning, the path, the way. Take time with it and enjoy it. It will come to you, and you'll know it by your conclusion that it's probable (if followed) and makes sense. The plan may not be easy, but the first step sure better be!

Finally, don't overplay or underplay execution. Great execution on a bad plan will get you bad results. However, the opposite is true too. Poor execution on a great plan will get you bad results. The trick is in the plan itself. You probably already know how hard it is to strike out when your strategy doesn't really make sense. Get a plan that you can believe in, then get after that first step. That's the way you build momentum, experience progress, feel happiness, and get to where you want to be.

Chapter 11 Takeaways

- The next step is never hard.
- Planning is just putting together the path of steps, starting with the easiest!
- Ask: How can the goal be reached?
    - What are the possible paths?
    - What would be a good organizing metaphor?
    - What are the logical steps to reach the goal?
    - What is the probability of success if you follow your plan?

Chapter 12

Enjoying Problems as a Way of Life

Why should you enjoy problems as a way of life? The answer is that it's the path away from anxiety and toward motivation and happiness. Well, I should say it points to the path, the path that is happiness step-by-step.

> **Mandalorian**: *This is the way. Why would one choose to relish in difficulties as a way of existence? The response is simple: it's the course that leads away from apprehension and towards incentive and contentment. Allow me to clarify, it reveals the path, the path that leads towards success and one step at a time. You must learn to embrace problems as the means to all honor and progress. So, remember, a warrior challenges the obstacle because it is on the path. This is the way.*

I shared this list earlier, but now I want to invite you to think about it a little bit deeper. Thinking clearly about problems will help you enjoy them for life. Feel free to add your reasons to the list.

1. Problems lead to happiness.

It's hard to avoid the importance and desire we have toward happiness. A lot of philosophy rummages through all kinds of discarded theories. I'll just tell you how I see it, but you'll have to work this through for yourself. I believe you are happy when you think the present will lead to the future you want. Of course, if you don't want anything in the future, then you are already there! This is why detachment can have a calming and happifying effect. If what is happening in this moment (the present) is going to get you what you want (the future), then any progress is going to feel good. Now add to that an understanding of unhappiness. Unhappiness is when you think the present will lead to a future you don't want. By definition, that's what a problem is, that which hinders your happiness. Problems make all of this clear to us. They define happiness in the future, what's in the way, and what needs to be done to get there. Every step toward your solution to a problem you notice will allow you to experience a little burst of happiness.

2. Problems motivate us.

Following from #1, motivation starts with unhappiness and ends with happiness. Face it, if you were totally happy about everything in life, in your world, and in your business, why would you take any action at all? You wouldn't. Every bit of motivation comes down to some kind of focus on solving a problem to get to what you want. You can be motivated to act or avoid acting, but both are defined by the problem lessening because of what you do (or don't). If you need motivation, just find a solvable problem that will lead to a future you want.

3. Problems make money.

Money is a medium for exchanging value. Instead of finding someone who needs a goat (which I have) and has an extra anvil-and-hammer (which I want), I can sell my goat for money and use that money to buy my anvil-and-hammer. So, how does that relate to problems? Everyone is giving others their money to solve one or more problems. Why do you buy food, disinfectant, a car, a parachute, or a costume for Halloween? All of them involve solving a problem. Even purchasing stocks or going to see a movie is meant to solve some kind of problem, sometimes unique to the individual. When you enjoy problems, and solve them for others, they will gladly pay you. Of course,

4. Problems seek solutions.

The moment you want something and realize what's in the way, is also the moment some kind of solution will come to mind. As we know, this process can easily get misguided because we don't define things well. Nonetheless, the nature of a problem moves us to look for a solution, just as a question moves us to find an answer. Questions are problems that want to be answered, that's how it works. Cool, huh?

5. Problems create jobs.

Everyone has been hired to solve some kind or kinds of problems. From receptionist to wide receiver, you are there to solve something. When you hire people, isn't it to solve a problem? Leaders are job creators because they are problem lovers. When you see problems, you might as well see jobs! If you want to make a job or team obsolete, then just figure out how your problems can be solved without it.

6. Problems give us purpose.

It goes with happiness, but it's deeper in our spirits. Setting out on a quest to end some injustice is the hallmark of the hero's journey. When you find a problem that captures your heart, you'll find purpose. If you solve it in your lifetime, you'll need to look for another one!

7. Problems create customers.

In a sense, this reason is the same as the one about money. Customers can be bosses or board members, not just buyers. Customers give you money, but that's not all. There is something wonderfully human about someone appreciating what you've done for them, even when they've paid for it. Problems that we solve for people are what makes them into customers. Often, the reason you don't have more customers is that they either don't know that you exist, or you haven't explained to them the problem you solve for them.

8. Problems grow skills.

If you have skills, then they came about by practice motivated by problems. Pick any skill of yours and you'll see the point. If a skill is a means to overcome a problem you care about, then you will develop the skill if you are going to win. I am a skilled swimmer. In the deep south, if you didn't swim you didn't have many friends. We had a lake cabin, a pool membership, and vacationed on the Gulf Coast. So much of our summer was consumed with swimming, such that you had to get good at it just to keep up. If you aren't good at selling, so what? It's a problem, learn the skill.

9. Problems show us our strengths.

Sometimes we just don't know what we have inside until a crisis calls. A crisis is just a big, immediate problem. Leadership potential is one of the more obvious strengths that displays itself in a difficult moment. Team and company difficulties can also show you what we're made of, and once you know you can use it as a force for good.

10. Problems reveal our weaknesses.

In a similar way, problems can reveal our weaknesses. Weaknesses are a call to grow a skill or to get more help. Problems beautifully help us to quit pretending we can do things we can't. Of course, that doesn't mean the cause is lost, but rather that the focus needs to adjust.

11. Problems create goals.

The entire book has largely been about this point. A problem, when well considered, points us toward a goal that will save the day when reached. Several years back, I had a high calcium score (a debatable tool used to predict heart problems) which prompted me to solve my worries about my heart. With some family history of heart disease, I began to study the topic. Basically, I set a new goal to get my heart to a state of 'as healthy as possible'. I switched to a plant-based (avoid oils) diet and began running about three miles daily. As of today, I weigh 50 pounds less than my peak weight and my resting heart rate is 40 bps. It could all be over tomorrow, but the problem created a goal as a solution. And yet, I've talked to my doctors about this stuff…it's all good!

12. Problems show us what we want.

In some ways, this is the most valuable thing about problems. I'm one given to not really knowing what I want, because I tend to think I want everything. They say that optimists think the glass is half-full, while pessimists think the glass is half-empty. I think the glass is half mine! However, when I see something that bothers me enough to consider it a problem, it directs me to what I really want. In the example above, having a potential heart problem clarified for me how much I wanted to get done in this life. So, now I've committed to retire when I turn 80 (over a decade and a half away). Honestly, when I get there, depending on how I'm doing, I might just re-enlist to do more until I'm 90!

13. Problems create plans.

Since a problem can show us what we want and create a goal for us to pursue, it's only natural to understand that the plan grows from the problem as well. It's only natural, once you have a goal you want in mind, to start working on some kind of game plan. Basically, we can say no problems, no goals, no plans, no action. Or, we can say it the other way around.

14. Problems inspire creativity.

Yes, inventiveness is a big part of crafting solutions. Problems inspire creativity. Using our imagination and paying attention to a thing is the heart of the secret. Once we have a defined problem and a goal to solve it, our minds want to start coming up with options about how to see the solution into reality. You are largely creative when you are clear about what you are trying to create, which at some level, is about moving from an unhappy problem to a happy solution.

15. Problems multiply learnings.

Every experience with working on a solution adds to your fund of knowledge and grows some of your skills. As a minister, I easily averaged a speech (45 minutes or more) every week for 25 years. That comes out to 1,300 speeches. I'm pretty sure that solving all the problems in understanding the topic and organizing my thoughts multiplied my learnings. There is no doubt that the knowledge and skills I have would not be there without those 1,300 problems (what do I tell them this week?)!

16. Problems unite people.

Perhaps nothing is more obvious than how problems unite people. From a revolutionary war to a family crisis, focusing on the problem tends to move everyone closer together. With couples, if they think the other person is the problem then there is nothing but conflict. On the other hand, if they conclude together that the relationship is the problem, then they have something to work on together. Bear in mind that while problems unite, solutions can sometime divide. What kind of country should we have? That roughly unites two groups who are not united, which is sort of the idea. In your business, however, having a clear goal to solve an agreed-upon problem will almost always unite the team. You can enjoy problems for that reason as well.

17. Problems exist anyway, why not enjoy them?

Yes, it is a problem-filled world. You've had them since the moment you were born. You'll have them until the last breath you take. Why not go ahead and enjoy them? They are simply a part of reality, but they are generated by your desire for things to change to suit you (who said people don't like change?). The things that aren't real problems can be dropped, and the real problems that exist can be solved. Why not go ahead and get hooked on solving these things? You have the manual before you and seventeen other reasons enjoying problems is the way to go. Again, problems are a part of reality. You are welcome to get in a brawl with her, but Reality never tires, quits, or loses. Just team up with her and enjoy the things that problems give you, plus the happiness a solution realized brings.

Finally, start proclaiming, "Excellent...a problem seeking a solution! Let's help them meet." Or something like that, including something as simple as, "I Enjoy Problems!"

Chapter 12 Takeaways

- Thinking clearly about problems will help you enjoy them for life.
- There are at least 17 reasons to enjoy problems, including the fact that they exist anyway. Why not go ahead and enjoy them?
- Feel free to add your reasons to the list.

CONCLUSION

How To Become
A Solutions-Crafting Wizard

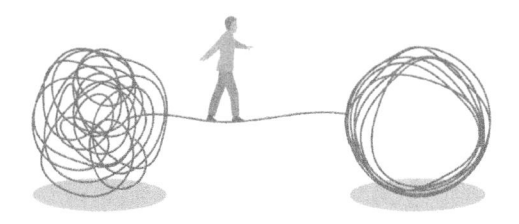

What to Do Next

You can become a wizard. You have more than you need to get on the path to becoming a powerful solution-crafter. No matter how good you are already, if you tweak your approach to include what you've been introduced to here, everything will change for the better. I promise.

> **Mandalorian**: *This is the way, my friend. You have the potential to become a sorcerer of some renown. You possess more than enough to embark on the journey to becoming a mighty solutions-crafter. Regardless of how skilled you may already be, incorporating what you have learned here into your way will change everything for the better. I give you my word. This is the way.*

Do you remember the old saying about being a "Jack of All Trades, But a Master of None" as an insult? If you study the history of it, you'll find that it was meant as a profound complement. The original saying was something like, "A jack of all trades is a master of none, but oftentimes better than a master of one." This person could come to a village and fix any number of problems he encountered. He was a generalist and an integrator. You might even say he was a polymath (multiple learner). That's a lot of what makes up the spirit of the leader. You are just a master at solving problems in a lot of different areas. Every problem is an opportunity to practice and learn a little more. Here are the basics we covered.

- Problems are everywhere, and they are wonderful.
- Quit solving problems, craft solutions.
- Leaders are the heroes of problem-solving.
- Most people problem-soothe instead of problem-solve.
- The only two ways to end a problem.
    o Achieve a solution.
    o Quit wanting what creates the problem.
- Anxiety prevents creative problem-solving, so it must be addressed first.
- When the problem is gone, the anxiety is gone.
- Problems must be defined carefully.
- The superior path is to look for permanent solutions to your pressing problems.
- Some things aren't problems, they are just reality.
- A solid process is better than a silly brainstorm.
- When you are skilled at solving them, problems will be one of your joys.
- The solution to any problem is just a goal.

Just for emphasis, I want to add a point about looking for permanent solutions. George Polya in his book *How to Solve It*, basically said, "The more ambitious plan may have a greater chance of success." I think there is something to that. It is reaching beyond the common to the special, which engages our greatest creative talents. Polya also points out that Pascal was aiming for a universal method of problem solving (my secret passion), which seems to make him reach beyond the ordinary to the extraordinary. When you look for a permanent, eternal solution, you really can't get more ambitious. Can you? There is more to it, but you have what you need here. At least begin using Business Casual, but don't undervalue the power of the Full Monty. It's the most comprehensive and flexible approach. You are on your way to your next level. Take out a problem and walk through the process. Put in a little time and you'll see with new eyes. If you want help getting there faster and better, just contact us through EnjoyingProblems.com.

-Dr. Fred

If you'd like to build some trust, we have a couple of courses that are 100% free for book owners at enjoyingproblems.com/bookbonuses. You'll notice I use a lot of QUESTIONS throughout this book. One free course which helps you create better questions for better results. The second course is a recorded live training on the Simple6 Method. There's no pushy sales-pitch or upsell. I want you to get better so your future will be better.

Appendix A: Fear as a Friend

Do you think in opposites? You really need to. It will change your life. It's not an all-the-time thing, but it is extremely valuable. You might have noticed by now that this really is an opposite book. I'm challenging you to enjoy problems rather than hating and avoiding them. Some of the best money advice I ever received was an opposite. "To get wealthy, just study what poor people do and do the opposite." It may be an overstatement and isn't fair to the plight of the real poor, but there is some insight there.

Fear is decidedly in need of some opposite thinking. Fear should be our friend. The common way to think is that fear is bad, and you should learn to be a fearless trailblazer. Actually, if you are 100% fearless, you are 100% stupid. Let me show you why.

Fear is really the path to wisdom. All the great wisdom literature is about the consequences of life choices. If you don't fear a bad outcome, how can you become wise or learn anything? The opposite of wisdom is foolishness. Here's an example from Proverbs 29:12 (NCV),

> **If a ruler pays attention to lies,**
> **all his officers will become wicked.**

Basically, this is saying that what gets rewarded gets done. It applies to children and employees and terrorists. If you listen enough to whining (employees or kids), then you'll just get more whining. If you are not afraid of the consequences of whining, then you'll just carry on until the trouble becomes unbearable. Fear of outcomes gives us the proper focus to be wise in our decisions. Of course, there are extremes. You can be so overcome with fear that you can't act. This is why anxiety is an understandable, yet dangerous, issue for leaders. One of the ways I like to think through a topic is to write aphorisms. Aphorisms are short observations about a truth, said in a memorable way. For example, 'the bigger they are, the harder they fall'. Here are a few aphorisms of mine about the importance of seeing fear as good.

1. The only thing to fear is something worth fearing.
2. A fool is afraid of the wrong things.
3. A wise person is afraid of the right things.
4. All fear is the fear of getting what you do not want.
5. A goal achieved is a fear relieved.
6. Stuck means stuck between two fears you think are equal.

7. Between two fears, the one you fear the most will win.
8. The chief goal is to remove your fear and enjoy its absence.
9. When someone is upset, just ask yourself, "What are they afraid of?"
10. When you are upset, just ask yourself, "What am I afraid of?" Then ask, "What else?"
11. Not everyone fears the same thing, because not everyone wants the same thing.
12. All fear is prediction. So, when you don't predict, you can't fear.

Do you get the idea? I find pondering these kinds of things to be extremely helpful. You may not agree or understand them all, but that's the beauty of reflection. My point is that fear is a normal part of life and can be a great contributor to our growth. Your anxiety is caused by predicting things about the future and not creating a proper hierarchy. We've showed you how to conquer both in this book, but you'll need to work at it as a skill to grow. For clarity, what I mean by hierarchy is illustrated by a passer-by who goes into a burning building to rescue someone trapped inside. You can pretend that they are fearless, but you'd miss what's really happening. People generally fear burning to death. When a person goes into a fire to rescue someone, they are simply more afraid of the person dying than they are of themselves dying. In this way there is a hierarchy, one fear overcomes the other. As you grow, you'll see the power of dismissing false fears and embracing real ones. Next, you'll figure out how to get them organized to make your life better and wiser.

Are you more afraid of losing a customer or an employee? If I know which you fear the most, I can predict what you'll do if they show up at the same time. Of course, you could fear conflict so much that you avoid dealing with either. Ah, the joys of anxiety!

I assure you that you can grow in wisdom and befriend your fears. If you'd like help in fast-tracking these skills, go to EnjoyingProblems.com.

Appendix B: Anxiety Outthinker Checklist

DR. FRED'S HANDY-DANDY ANXIETY OUTTHINKER CHECKLIST
(TO BE PRACTICED)

- ✓ How anxious do I feel? [1-10 scale]
- ✓ Do I clearly know what I feel anxious about happening in the future? What's the story?
- ✓ Am I anxious or just excited (or a little of both)? Assume 'excitement' when possible. It's often hard to distinguish between the two.
- ✓ Is what I'm actually anxious about happening now in real time? Really?
- ✓ Do I really think I know the future?

  - Am I a prophet or prophetess?
  - What 2 or 3 other stories could possibly happen?

- Are my hopes of good things happening in the future clear in my mind?
  - What do I want?
  - What will it feel like if what I want happens?
  - Can I easily picture this story of what I want?

✓ Do I now notice my anxiety has lessened? [1-10 scale]

Appendix C: The Full Monty

Here are the specific steps in our framework as a series of strategic questions:

SEEK

1. What do you think the problem is right now?
2. What are you most afraid of if this problem wins?
   a) Why is that a problem?
   b) Why else?

3. What do you want to happen?
   a) Why that?
   b) Why that?
   c) What happens if you win here?

4. How would you now define the real problem given what you want?

SEE

5. What are the relevant pieces or elements?
6. What else do you see that might relate?
   a) What else?
   b) Is the problem, or any of its elements, unchangeable realities?

SORT

7. How would you sort the pieces into appropriate categories or groups?

SIMPLIFY

8. What is the flow, the logic, of how it all works?

SOLVE

9. What goal, if reached, would solve the problem forever?
   a) Why would it solve it?
   b) What else might work?
   c) Why would that solve it?
   d) What's the better goal?

10. How can the goal be reached?
    a) What are the possible paths?
    b) What would be a good organizing metaphor?
    c) What are the logical steps to reach the goal?
    d) What would you guess is the probability of success if you follow your plans?

SIMULATE

11. Check: Is there a good chance this is just a Reality that can't be solved? If yes, then are you attacking the wrong problem?
12. Imagine the solution being fully implemented and working at full capacity. What happens? What's good? What accidentally happens that is bad?
13. What is the Best-Case Scenario? The Worse-Case Scenario? The Most-Likely Scenario?
14. What five factors would make a good Score Card? What grade would you give each area on how well the goal will solve the problem? What overall grade would you give the goal?

Appendix D: Business Casual

1. What do you think is the problem?
   a) Why is that a problem?
   b) Why is that a problem?

2. What do you want to happen?
   a) Why that?
   b) Why that?
   c) What happens if you win here?
   d) How would you now define the real problem?

3. What goal, if accomplished, would solve this problem forever?

   a) Why would it work?

4. How can the goal be reached?

   a) What are the major steps necessary for reaching the goal?

   b) What's the next step?

   c) When will you promise to complete the next step by?

About the Author

Dr. Fred Ray Lybrand Jr.

Dr. Lybrand has been married to Jody for over 43 years, and together they have five children who were home-educated until college (they are all college grads, married, and have 11 kids between them). His lifelong pursuit has been toward formulating a universal problem-solving model, which he calls the Simple6 Model. His diverse experiences include The University of Alabama (BA in English Literature/Communications/Fiction-Writing), Speech Communication Instructor (University of Alabama), Law School (University of Alabama), an MA in Biblical Studies (Dallas Theological Seminary), and a Doctorate in Applied Theology (Phoenix Seminary).

In his own words he's a Communicator, a Solutions-Catalyst, a Problems-Optimist, and a Simplifier. He has authored 12 books and several academic papers. Lybrand's experience includes government, energy, biotech, robotic automation, securities, small business, healthcare, and more. His client list includes the US Air Force, US Space Force, State Farm Insurance, Valero, Chick-fil-A, Pioneer Natural Resources, Encana, Marathon Oil, Rose & Associates, ProTrader, Burlington Resources, Continental Oil, AcuFocus, Maplewood Investment Partners, Connally Plumbing, Inc., Midland Country Club, Silver Creek Oil & Gas, Infinity Concrete Construction, Westhill Paving, Talentum Engineering, PTX Therapy, and 3DPlans.com. Besides a myriad of certifications in personality and communication-effectiveness testing, Dr. Lybrand has been a long-term student of structural and systems dynamics. A couple of distinctions worth mentioning are his Organizational Consultant Certification with Robert Fritz, Inc. (mentor to Peter Senge, Sloan School of Management @ MIT) & 'Best of the Best Honoree Award' (American Society of Safety Engineers) for his two-part article on *Transcendent Leadership*.

Bonuses To Enjoy

ENJOYING PROBLEMS comes with 2 Bonuses that you can gain access to by registering your ownership of the book. Here's what's waiting for you:

1. The 3 Essential Infographics in a printable Quick Reference format:
     - Dr. Fred's Handy-Dandy Anxiety Outthinker Checklist
     - The Full Monty (Simple6 Model)
     - Business Casual (QuickStart Version of the Simple6 Model)
2. Free Access to a 1.5 hour live-recorded training on the essentials of the Simple6 Method (video and audio).
3. Free Access to our course on how to improve your Question-Making Skill as a leader.
4. A surprise.

GO HERE: enjoyingproblems.com/bookbonuses

Additional Resources

WARNING & HOPE: In full disclosure, our process engages several micro-skills, which you probably already have in some measure. A micro-skill is like putting in golf. It's essential, but it isn't the whole game. However, improving it (or any micro-skill) improves everything.

We offer more in-depth training on these, but you are going to have so much leverage with our framework, you'll probably do just fine.

Here is the list our consultants/coaches/students will learn master: Logic * Whole Picture Thinking (S4) * Solutions Thinking * Strategic Thinking (Ockham's Lever) * Communication Thinking * Mathematical Thinking * Motivation & Goal-Setting * Visual Thinking * Language Thinking * Emotions Mastery * Lazy Thinking (Systems) * Idea Generation * Insight Journaling * Heuristics/Principles/

PMM/Metaphors * Synthetic/Divergent Thinking. If you'd like to learn about our additional training, just drop us a note at support@enjoyingproblems.com

Made in the USA
Coppell, TX
25 October 2024